PADDLE STEAMERS

AT WAR 1939-1945

This book, published to coincide with the 50th Anniversary of the end of World War Two, commemorates the part played in it by British paddle steamers and is intended as a tribute to the men who served aboard, or were rescued by them.

Many of the photographs are from the Imperial War Museum collection, or individuals, and acknowlegement of source is given where known.

Compiled and Edited by
Russell Plummer

CONTENTS

Left: A midships close-up of the Campbell veteran *Westward Ho*
(Richard Howarth Collection)

INTRODUCTION

Over 50 paddle steamers were called up for service with the Royal Navy during the Second World War, many of them answering the call to duty for a second time after performing a variety of tasks between 1914 to 1918. The first steamers were requisitioned within a few days of war being declared on 3rd September 1939 and by early 1940 some 30 vessels had been commissioned to supplement the Royal Navy's purpose-built minesweepers. The paddlers were formed into five flotillas: the 7th, seven vessels based at Granton, on the Forth; the 8th, five vessels at North Shields; the 10th, eight ships at Dover; the 11th, five steamers on the Clyde at Greenock; and the 12th, five vessels and based at Harwich.

Conversion work, carried out in quick time by both naval dockyards and by private shipyards, fitted the paddlers for minesweeping using Oropesa equipment consisting of twin torpedo shaped floats, carried aft and streamed astern using a system of kites and with cutters to sever mooring cables to release mines where they were exploded by rifle or gun fire. For armament the paddlers were fitted with a single 12 pounder gun forward and lighter anti-aircraft pieces, usually Lewis guns, on the paddle boxes or sponsons. Some skippers showed great ingenuity in obtaining additional weapons and the paddle minesweepers were capable of putting up a substantial if not always particularly well directed barrage.

Although the Clyde-based 11th Flotilla consisted of 1930s-built steamers - sisters *Caledonia* and *Mercury,* and *Juno* and *Jupiter* from Caledonian Steam Packet's Gourock fleet and the London and North Eastern Railway's *Jeanie Deans* from the north bank at Craigendoran - the other four groups included a cross-section with units ranging in age from a few years to veterans built in the 1890s,

the 10th flotilla at Dover including, for example, two of the famous Belle steamers, the *Laguna Belle* of 1896 and *Thames Queen* of 1898, plus the *Emperor of India* of 1906 and ships built as recently as *Sandown* (1934) and the *Gracie Fields* of 1936.

The three largest Thames excursion paddlers from the Eagle Steamers fleet, *Royal Eagle, Crested Eagle* and *Golden Eagle,* were designated Thames Special Service ships and fitted from the outset to act in an anti-aircraft role armed with two single 2 pounder A/A guns, six 20mm A/A guns, 2 Lewis Guns, 12 x .303 machine guns in quadruple Boulton and Paul turrets and two four barrel rocket projectors.

This trio were among over 20 paddlers to take part in the evacuation of the British Expeditionary Force from Dunkirk in a nine day operation from 26th May 1940. Between them the steamers, including two taken off Isle of Wight ferry services and sent across unarmed, were responsible for returning almost 26,000 troops but the cost was high with six paddlers lost. From 1941, as the naval building programme augmented the minesweeping fleet, many of the paddle sweepers underwent conversion to auxiliary anti-aircraft ships with some of the older steamers relegated to training or accommodation ship status. Additional paddlers were requisitioned and converted for use as A/A ships and by 1943, only a three ship Granton minesweeping flotilla remained. The A/A steamers were concentrated in the Thames Estuary and, as the build up to the Normandy Landings gathered pace, along the South Coast. A number of paddlers fulfilled key roles on D-Day and in the period immediately afterwards and, later in 1944, several vessels appeared in the Schelde Estuary for the liberation of Holland and Belgium.

VESSELS REQUISITIONED FOR WAR SERVICE 1939-45

Listed here are all paddle steamers known to have been commissioned into the Royal Navy from September 1939 onwards, plus other vessels requisitioned from civilian services to take part in the Dunkirk evacuation in 1940. Where names were changed during hostilities, the original name appears beneath. Pennant numbers prefixed 'J' relating to minesweeping were changed to numbers officially prefixed '4' for steamers later converted to an anti-aircraft role. In some cases the letter 'R' was substituted for figure '4.' At the beginning of the war some of the minesweepers also carried pennant numbers with the prefix 'N'. The vessels are arranged under headings of the areas where they operated before the war.

Clyde and Western Isles

Vessel	Built	GRT	Owner	War role	Pen.No.
ARISTOCRAT (TALISMAN)	1935	544	London & North Eastern Rly.	A/A vessel; Normandy HQ ship at Arromanches 1944; handed back 1946; returned to service 1947-66.	4-200
DUCHESS OF FIFE	1903	336	Caledonian Steam Packet	Minesweeper 12th Flotilla; later training vessel on the Forth; handed back 1946; returned to service 1946-53.	J.115
DUCHESS OF ROTHESAY	1894	338	Caledonian Steam Packet	Minesweeper; accommodation ship 1942; handed back 1946; not reconditioned, broken-up 1947.	J.107
FAIR MAID	1886	211	Grangemouth and Forth Towing Co.	Requisitioned 1940, allocated to the Clyde for harbour duty. Fitted as decontamination vessel. Released and scrapped 1945.	-
GOATFELL (CALEDONIA)	1934	624	Caledonian Steam Packet	Minesweeper 11th Flotilla; A/A vessel from 1942, handed back 1945; returned to service 1946-69; static use in London 1971-79.	J.125 4-36
GONDOLIER	1886	173	David MacBrayne	Requisitioned November 1939. Engine, boiler & Sponsons removed before hull towed to Scapa Flow to be sunk & used as blockship on 23rd March 1940.	-
HARLEQUIN (STRATHMORE)	1897	316	Caledonian Steam Packet	Converted for use as Accomodation ship at Chatham in June 1942. Wrecked on passage to the Clyde in March 1943.	-
HARBINGER (PIONEER)	1905	241	David MacBrayne	Requisitioned 1944 as submarine HQ ship, Fairlie Purchased by Admiralty 1945 used 1946-58 as research ship at Portland Harbour.	-
HELVELLYN (JUNO)	1937	642	Caledonian Steam Packet	Minesweeper 11th Flotilla; bombed in London during conversion to A/A ship 20th March 1941, declared constructive total loss.	J.120
JEANIE DEANS	1931	636	London & North Eastern Rly.	Minesweeper 11th Flotilla; converted to A/A ship in 1941; handed back 1944; returned to service 1946-64, 1966-67.	J.108 4-29

A remarkable view of the *Kylemore* following conversion for service as a netlayer. The upper deck has been extended to the stern with substantial davits fitted on either beam to handle booms and buoyant barriers. The vessel was sunk by bombing off Harwich in August 1940
(Clyde River Steamer Club).

KYLEMORE	1897	318	Caledonian Steam Packet	Minesweeper; converted to Netlayer and lost on 21st August 1940 by aerial bombing off Harwich.	-
MARMION	1906	406	London & North Eastern Rly.	Minesweeper 12th Flotilla; at Dunkirk; bombed sunk by bombing at Harwich on 9th April 1941, raised but declared constructive total loss.	J.114
MERCURY	1934	621	Caledonian Steam Packet	Minesweeper 11th Flotilla, sunk after damage by own mine south of Ireland, 25th December 1940.	J.102
ORIOLE (EAGLE III)	1910	441	Williamson-Buchanan	Minesweeper 12th Flotilla; took part in Dunkirk evacuation; accommodation ship from 1944 handed back 1945; not reconditioned, broken-up 1946.	J.ll0
QUEEN EMPRESS	1912	411	Williamson-Buchanan	Minesweeper 12th Flotilla- converted to A/A ship 1942; handed back 1944; not reconditioned, broken-up 1946.	J.128 4-399
SCAWFELL (JUPITER)	1937	642	Caledonian Steam Packet	Minesweeper 11th Flotilla; A/A vessel 1941, handed back 1945; returned to service 1946-57.	J.103 4-22
WAVERLEY	1899	537	London & North Eastern Rly.	Minesweeper 12th Flotilla; sunk by aerial bombs returning from Dunkirk, 29th May 1940.	J.51

Bristol Channel

Vessel	Built	GRT	Owner	War role	Pen.No.
DEVONIA	1905	520	P & A.Campbell Bristol	Minesweeper 7th Flotilla; deliberately beached after bomb damage at La Panne, near Dunkirk, 31st May 1940.	J.113
GLEN AVON	1912	509	P & A.Campbell Bristol	Minesweeper 8th Flotilla; at Dunkirk, later A/A vessel and in Normandy Landings; lost during storm in Bay of the Seine, 2nd September 1944.	J.104 4-392
GLEN GOWER	1922	553	P & A.Campbell Bristol	Minesweeper (SO ship 10th Flotilla); at Dunkirk; A/A vessel renamed *GLENMORE* 1942; handed back 1945; returned to service 1947-57.	J.16 4-368
GLEN USK	1914	524	P & A.Campbell Bristol	Minesweeper 8th Flotilla; A/A vessel from 1942; examination vessel Normandy Landings; handed back 1945; returned to service 1946-60.	J.26 4-377
PLINLIMMON (CAMBRIA)	1895	438	P & A.Campbell Bristol	Minesweeper 7th Flotilla; one trip to Dunkirk; A/A vessel from 1942; accommodation ship 1944, then laid-up London Docks until gutted by fire, broken-up 1947.	J.66 4-335
RAVENSWOOD	1891	391	P & A.Campbell Bristol	Requisitioned 1942 as A/A ship; handed back 1945, returned to service 1946-54.	4-328
SKIDDAW (BRITANNIA)	1896	459	P & A.Campbell Bristol	Minesweeper 7th Flotilla; converted to A/A ship 1942; handed back 1945; returned to service 1945-56.	J.80 4-301
SNAEFELL (WAVERLEY)	1907	477	P & A.Campbell Bristol	Minesweeper 8th Flotilla; present at Dunkirk; sunk by aerial bombing off the River Tyne, 5th July 1941.	J.118
WESTWARD HO	1894	438	P & A.Campbell Bristol	Minesweeper 8th Flotilla; at Dunkirk; converted to A/A ship 1942; accommodation role from 1944; released and broken-up 1946.	J.43 4-390

Four views from the Richard Howarth collection showing vessels from the P & A.Campbell fleet immediately after war service. The *Westward Ho* is seen (above, left) in Cumberland Basin, Bristol, in 1946 shortly before being sold for scrap; the *Ravenswood* (above right) was more fortunate being returned to service as were *Glen Gower,* ex *HMS Glenmore* (below left) undergoing reconditioning at the Charles Hill yard, Bristol, and *Glen Usk* (below, right) steaming up the River Avon past Sea Mills when returning to Bristol on 4th October 1945.

Weymouth and Bournemouth

Vessel	Built	GRT	Owner	War role	Pen.No.
AMBASSADOR (EMBASSY)	1911	318	Cosens & Co. Weymouth	Minesweeper; training ship from 1944; handed back 1945; returned to service 1946-66.	J.109
CONSUL	1896	277	Cosens & Co. Weymouth	Requisitioned in November 1939 and used until November 1944 for patrol and examination work at Portland. Returned to service 1948-64.	-
EMPEROR OF INDIA	1906	534	Cosens and Co. Weymouth	Minesweeper 10th Flotilla; A/A vessel 1940; accommodation ship (named *BUNTING*) from July 1945; handed back 1946; returned to service 1948-56.	J.106 4-273
EMPRESS	1879	173	Cosens and Co. Weymouth	Requisioned September 1939 and used as examination vessel to January 1941 and from March to November 1944. Returned to service 1946-55.	-
EXWAY (MONARCH)	1888	315	Cosens and Co. Weymouth	Used from November 1939 to November 1944 as examination vessel mainly at Portland and later at Portsmouth. Returned 1945, in service 1946-50.	-
VICTORIA	1884	229	Cosens & Co. Weymouth	Used from August 1939 to November 1944 on examination and control duties. Returned to excursion sailings 1946-53.	-

After initially serving as a minesweeper, the *Emperor of India* is seen here after conversion to serve as an anti-aircraft vessel towards the end of 1940 when based at Harwich *(IWM)*.

Southampton and Portsmouth

Vessel	Built	GRT	Owner	War role	Pen.No.
BALMORAL	1900	471	Red Funnel Southampton	A/A vessel; accommodation ship on the Clyde at Greenock 1943; handed back 1946; not reconditioned, broken-up 1949.	4-241

Balmoral, hardly recognisable as an accommodation ship on the River Clyde in 1945. Returned to Red Funnel at Southampton it was not deemed fit for further service *(Graham Langmuir).*

Despite looking a little neglected at Weymouth in 1945, the *Victoria,* powered by an oscillating engine, was put back into the excursion trade by Cosens and Co. and can be seen here blending into the background! *(Bernard Cox).*

Photographs of Cosens' *Embassy* in war service as *HMS Ambassador* are few and far between. Here the one time Portsmouth railway steamer is seen at Weymouth *(Richard Howarth collection).*

BOURNEMOUTH QUEEN	1908	428	Red Funnel Southampton	Requisitioned as A/A vessel 1942; accommodation ship at Fort William 1943; handed back 1947; returned to service 1948-57.	4-270
FRESHWATER	1927	264	Southern Railway	Examination ship at Portland. Reported sent to Dunkirk evacuation but not officially listed as taking part; later at Portsmouth; released 1946 remained in service until 1961.	-
GRACIE FIELDS	1936	393	Red Funnel Southampton	Minesweeper 10th Flotilla, sank 29th May 1940 after being bombed returning from second trip to Dunkirk.	J.100
LORNA DOONE	1891	410	Red Funnel Southampton	Minesweeper 12th Flotilla; converted to A/A ship 1942; accommodation role at Greenock from 1943; handed back 1947; not reconditioned, broken-up 1949.	J.135 4-402
PORTSDOWN	1928	342	Southern Railway	Requisitioned solely to take part in the Dunkirk evacuation, handed back immediately afterwards. Sunk by mine in Spithead, 20th September 1941.	-
PRINCESS ELIZABETH	1927	371	Red Funnel Southampton	Minesweeper 10th Flotilla; at Dunkirk- converted A/A ship from 1942; handed back 1944; returned returned to service 1946-65; static role London 1970-87; Paris since 1991.	J.111 4-403
RYDE	1937	603	Southern Railway	Minesweeper; converted to A/A vessel 1942; took part in Normandy Landings 1944; released 1945; returned to service 1945-69; still exists at Binfield, Isle of Wight.	J.132 4-39
SANDOWN	1934	684	Southern Railway	Minesweeper (SO ship 10th Flotilla); at Dunkirk; A/A vessel from 1942; handed back and returned to service 1945; withdrawn 1965, broken-up 1966.	J.20
SOUTHSEA	1930	825	Southern Railway	Minesweeper 8th Flotilla; mined 16th February 1941 off Tyne, beached but declared constructive total loss.	J.113
WHIPPINGHAM	1930	825	Southern Railway	Called from ferry service for Dunkirk operation; Requisitioned as minesweeper 1941; converted to A/A ship 1942; returned to service 1945-1962.	J.136 4-404

Sussex Coast

Vessel	Built	GRT	Owner	War role	Pen.No.
BRIGHTON BELLE	1900	320	P & A.Campbell Bristol	Minesweeper 10th Flotilla; lost after striking submerged wreck returning from Dunkirk, 25th May 1940.	J.117
BRIGHTON QUEEN	1905	519	P & A.Campbell Bristol	Minesweeper 10th Flotilla; lost following air attack returning from Dunkirk, 1st June 1940.	J.28

Above: *Lorna Doone* in two views after completing war service.
On the left the steamer is seen at Greenock with *Balmoral* alongside, and right, back at Southampton before being sold for scrap
(Richard Howarth collection).

Sandown, previously leader of the 10th Minesweeping Flotilla based at Dover, is pictured following conversion to serve as an anti-aircraft vessel in 1942.

After being called to Dunkirk, the *Whippingham* was not requisitioned for minesweeping until 1941 and became an anti-aircraft vessel the following year.

Thames and Medway

Vessel	Built	GRT	Owner	War role	Pen.No.
CITY OF ROCHESTER	1904	235	New Medway Steam Packet	Part converted as minesweeper, found unsuitable, designated store ship but sunk by aerial mine 19th May 1941, before entering service.	J.92
CRESTED EAGLE	1925	1110	General Steam Navigation Co.	A/A vessel from Thames Special Service Flotilla; lost at Dunkirk on 29th May 1940.	-
ESSEX QUEEN	1897	592	New Medway Steam Packet	Requisitioned as minesweeper; used as hospital ship 1940; handed back 1943; returned to service for Devon owners 1947-48.	J.101
GOLDEN EAGLE	1906	793	General Steam Navigation Co.	A/A vessel in Thames Special Service Flotilla; at Dunkirk; handed back 1945; returned to service 1947-49.	4-236
LAGUNA BELLE	1896	617	General Steam Navigation Co.	Minesweeper 10th Flotilla; converted to A/A ship 1942; accommodation vessel from 1943, released 1944, not reconditioned, broken-up 1946.	J.112 4-373
MEDWAY QUEEN	1924	318	New Medway Steam Packet	Minesweeper 10th Flotilla; made seven Dunkirk crossings; used as training ship from 1942; handed back and returned to service 1947-63; static use from 1966, now undergoing restoration.	J.48
QUEEN OF KENT	1916	798	New Medway Steam Packet	Built as minesweeper ATHERSTONE, converted for passenger use 1929; minesweeper 12th Flotilla 1939-44; handed back and returned to service 1946-51.	J.74
QUEEN OF THANET	1916	792	New Medway Steam Packet	Built as minesweeper MELTON, converted for passenger use 1929; SO vessel 10th Flotilla from 1940; present at Dunkirk; Control ship Selsey for Normandy Landings 1944; handed back and returned to service 1946-50.	J.30
ROYAL EAGLE	1932	1538	General Steam Navigation Co.	A/A vessel in Thames Special Service Flotilla; took part in Dunkirk evacuation; handed back 1945; returned to service 1946-50.	4-239
THAMES QUEEN	1898	517	New Medway Steam Packet	Minesweeper 10th Flotilla; A/A ship from 1942; then accommodation ship at Southampton until 1947 when handed back but not returned to service.	J.12 4-380

River Humber

Vessel	Built	GRT	Owner	War role	Pen.No.
KILLINGHOLME	1912	508	London & North Eastern Rly.	Requisitioned in May 1941 for service with Barrage Ballon Command at Grimsby. Released March 1945, withdrawn from use and scrapped.	-

Laguna Belle, originally the *Southend Belle* of 1896, and closely associated with the London-Clacton run in the 1930s, pictured following conversion to anti-aircraft vessel in 1943 *(IWM).*

Another famous 'Belle Steamer,' *Thames Queen* dating from 1898, served as an anti-aircraft vessel in the Thames Estuary and on the South Coast, latterly with this camouflage paintwork *(IWM).*

Used throughout the war for anti-aircraft duties, the large Thames steamer *Golden Eagle* brought back 1,751 men in three trips to Dunkirk during the 1940 evacuation. *Golden Eagle* survived the war to resume excursions from 1947 to 1949 *(IWM).*

City of Rochester in the River Medway after being sunk in May 1941 before going into service as a naval stores ship. Earlier, conversion to minesweeper started but the vessel was found unsuitable. *(Richard Howarth collection).*

Waverley and *Marmion,* pictured from the *Duchess of Fife,* returning to Harwich from one of the 12th Minesweeping Flotilla's patrols in the North Sea in April 1940, just a few weeks before all three vessels were called south to assist in the Dunkirk evacuation *(Rev. Wm. C. Galbraith collection).*

THE CLYDE STEAMERS AT WAR

During the first month of the war, the Government took over nine ships of the Clyde pleasure fleets. Most of the crews volunteered for service with their ships and remained in the Merchant service but came under Naval discipline. The captains were commissioned as navigating officers in the Royal Naval Reserve. They acted under commanding officers appointed by the Admiralty. The peace-time engineers were also commissioned and remained in charge below. The first assignment of the ship was to a refitting yard. There, engines were overhauled, and they swept the seats from the decks to make room for winches and minesweeping gear. Glass came out, and the windows were boarded up, while the comfortable upholstered lounges and cosy tea-rooms re-appeared as store-houses, miniature arsenals, hospitals or sleeping quarters for the crews and shops became wireless cabins or chart rooms.

When the Clyde steamers sailed out again, the gleaming hulls and the brightly painted funnel were beneath coats of warship grey. The 12 pounder gun on the bow and the Lewis gun mountings on each paddle box forewarned the crews that their voyages were no longer confined to points between Gourock or Craigendoran and the Kyles of Bute. The first steamer to leave the Clyde was the *Kylemore* built in the 1897 and a veteran of World War I which was again commissioned as a minesweeper.

On her bridge was Captain Fergus Murdoch of Greenock who told listeners: '*Kylemore* was fitted out in Greenock as a minesweeper and the first trip was to Ardrossan. There we had exercises, mostly gunnery practice. When instructions came through for us to proceed south, we stored and bunkered there. We

Based on the narrative for a documentary by W.R. ORR recording the gallant work of vessels of the River Clyde pleasure steamers fleet from 1939 to 1945 and broadcast by the Scottish Home Service on 25th October 1946.

set out in early November and for days the old ship ploughed her way through mountainous seas but the storm beat us and the *Kylemore* lost a paddle float. Eventually we reached Portsmouth and spent our first few weeks in working-up exercises. We practised sweeping mines off the Isle of Wight until we were posted to Dover as part of the 10th Minesweeping Flotilla - the only Clyde representative in it. The remainder were paddlers from the Thames, the South Coast and the Bristol Channel. There we soon discovered that sweeping was the easier part of the job.'

It was when mines were brought to the surface that the problems started as Captain Murdoch recalled: 'Their entire area is roughly a yard square. It keeps bobbing about, and often disappears from sight. A mere hit is not enough to sink the mine; you must hit the horns. That reduces the actual target to six inches by two. Nearly every man on the ship had a crack at our first mine. Finally we brought the ship round bow to the mine and trained the twelve pounder gun on it. We used nearly fifty shells before it disappeared. The crews of the flotilla chaffed us unmercifully over that incident. Our next incident wasn't so humorous, though. A mine fouled on the cutter. Usually, when its wire is broken, a mine comes to the surface. In this instance, the wire was caught, not broken, and we were actually trailing the mine along with us. We had to drag it for several miles to shallow water and then cut away the gear before exploding it. Our most thrilling experience was in the English Channel. As the *Kylemore* was the slowest ship in the flotilla our job was to destroy all mines swept.

'One mine exploded right below the ship. We thought we were goners for a moment. My first thoughts were for the CO who lay sick in the wardroom aft. He had been thrown off his settee and was laying badly bruised on the floor. His cabin was a shambles. So was mine. Furniture was smashed, charts and maps strewn around. My alarm clock lay in a thousand pieces on the floor. Luckily the hull of the ship was practically undamaged. The boilers suffered most, from leaking tubes but we struggled back to Dover without further incident.'

Five steamers of the pleasure fleets had been in Ardrossan to sound their farewells to the *Kylemore,* in the midst of their own training exercises. Within a few weeks, they, too, were sent south. The oldest ship of this little convoy was the *Duchess of Rothesay* built in 1895. Steaming beside her was the *Duchess of Fife,* similar in design but newer. Next in line was *HMS Oriole* a name that hid the identity of the Broomielaw favourite, the *Eagle III.* Two LNER ships accompanied them, the *Waverley* and the *Marmion.* All these vessels were veterans of the First World War. They arrived at Portsmouth on Christmas Eve 1939, and were later posted to form the major part of the 12th Minesweeping Flotilla based in Harwich. Meanwhile the fastest of the Clyde paddlers were commandeered to act with the 11th Minesweeping Flotilla after being briefly known as the 1st Flotilla. They began minesweeping near home, between Scotland and Ireland, from the Firth of Clyde to Rathlin Island. Another First World War veteran, the *Queen Empress* meanwhile sailed to Harwich to join the 12th Flotilla.

By the end of October 1939, 13 ships of the various Clyde fleets had been taken over for war duty. For months, they continued sweeping channels. The crews, veterans by now, found the routine task a trifle monotonous. Then in May, 1940, came the real war. Dunkirk! The *Jupiter* and the other members of the 11th Flotilla were in Rothesay Bay when they received the signal. They bunkered at once and steamed south. The Harwich-based 12th Flotilla were much nearer at hand so they were soon in action. The flagship, *Queen Empress,* was having an overhaul, and her place as Flotilla leader was taken by the *Waverley.* The *Marmion* sailed too with the peace-time skipper of the *Lucy Ashton,* Douglas McFarlane of Helensburgh, as navigating officer: 'The *Marmion* was coaling at Lowestoft when we were ordered to fill right up and proceed to a given position. There we met the remainder of the Flotilla. We had a hint of our eventual destination and most of us were keyed up at the thought of some real action. As we steamed south, vivid flashes lit the night sky and the sound of gunfire grew louder every minute. About midnight, we arrived off the little Belgian frontier town of La Panne. We lay off until daybreak. I'll never forget that sight. Ships of all sizes were crowded around us. Ashore, the beaches were black with troops. As there were no piers or jetties, we had to use our own lifeboats to get troops on board. A heavy surf pounding on the beaches made our job very difficult.

'Often the lifeboats were overturned, and the cries of the men thrown into the water added to the nightmare effect. All the time, the noise of the guns was rolling and always there would break-in the throb of German planes. The roar would get louder and louder, and then that sickening whistle and rush of falling bombs. The work of embarkation was slow. Luckily some Landing Craft (Personnel) arrived and they got our full complement on board. We were quite relieved to get away as air raids were becoming more frequent. We disembarked our troops in Dover and immediately began preparations for our second run. But the great air battle of the dauntless few had spread to our side of the Channel and we had to delay our departure until dusk. When we reached the Dunkirk beaches, the fighting was really intense. The Nazis sent their aircraft over dropping flares.

'We had to go right into Dunkirk Harbour and navigating that channel was the worst experience of my life. The night was pitch black. There were no buoy lights to guide me. I had to steer clear of the wrecks by the reflections from the blazing town itself and by the light of the flares overhead. The quayside was packed with British and French troops. We loaded as many as possible before the CO gave the order to shove the gangways off. I was glad to reach the open sea again. Luckily the weather had improved and the sea was like glass. We were all feeling exhausted during that trip back. We had been on our feet for more than 24 hours and had only had about two hours sleep in the last 48. We unloaded again in Dover and were instructed to prepare for a third run as dusk. All of us had a snooze in spite of the incessant bombing and machine-gunning.'

But it was another L.M.S. steamer, the *Eagle III*, that provided one of the highlights of the evacuation. Chief Engineer Robert Lindsay, of Port-Glasgow, was on board and this is his account of what happened: 'Like the others of the 12th Flotilla, we arrived off the beaches at Dunkirk in the middle of the night. Eventually we took the ship as close as possible and lowered our lifeboats. We hung rope ladders from the ship's railings. Our lifeboat were very unstable in the heavy surf, so most of the troops tried to wade out to the ship. As soon as they came past their depth, their heavy packs dragged them below the surface. Our crew did some wonderful life-saving work, but, unfortunately, we couldn't reach every one. They clambered aboard by any foothold they could find.

'We were very lucky. Ten bombs exploded all around the ship, but we had no casualties on board. The troops milled around our paddle boxes like bees. We just couldn't get the engines started. When the soldiers came aboard they were so exhausted they lay down in any spot they could find. In spite of the din all round them, many were sound asleep. The crew of the *Eagle III* carried out their mission of mercy for hours under bombing and machine-gunning. The gallant crew carried on, but, un-noticed, the tide was going out.' Not far away, another Clyde steamer the *Waverley* was busily engaged. Her Navigating Officer was Captain John Cameron, DSC, of Glasgow. He told listeners: 'As the *Waverley* drew into Dunkirk beaches ships were being blown up by mines all around us. The *Waverley*, however, with her shallow draft, got through safely. We lowered our lifeboats and fixed long ropes so that we could pull the troops out to the ship. Then the bombers got busy.

'Amid all this we tried towing the *Eagle* but there was no chance of getting her off the beaches. She was well aground. We did all we could until things became too hot for us. Our gunners kept blazing away at the raiding planes. Even the troops on board were sniping at them with their own rifles. Altogether, we brought down two planes - and that finished us. The Nazis gave us no peace after that. Twelve Heinkels fastened on us. They followed us as we steamed out to sea, diving all the time. We twisted and turned in all directions to escape the bombs and bullets. Then we had bad luck. A near miss damaged our rudder. The ship was out of control and, with so many mines about, we had to stop. The crew started to fix up a temporary rudder, but now we were a sitting target. We survived the first few bombs, and then we were struck amidships. That bomb got us just abaft of the engine room and exploded in the hospital, our old dinning room. It was hard to associate such a peaceful pre-war scene with the carnage that day.

Duchess of Fife, decks crowded with troops, gets underway from Dunkirk on one of three crossings she made during 'Operation Dynamo' at the end of May 1940, the steamer landing 1,801 troops in Margate and Dover *(Times Newspapers).*

The *Queen Empress,* leader of the Harwich Flotilla, missed Dunkirk due to an overhaul and is pictured later in the war carrying her anti-aircraft vessel pennant number *(IWM)*

'Three hundred men were killed or drowned. The blast splintered our lifeboats and made them useless. The ship was doomed and she began to settle in the water, so we got everything that would float and threw it overboard. The troops behaved magnificently, and many a lad sacrificed himself to help a wounded man on to the rafts. When I got away, the bridge was going under and I was sucked down by the ship. It seemed ages before I broke the surface. I couldn't swim, but luckily there was a raft nearby. I managed to catch one of the ropes and hung on. We were an hour and a half in the water before a small drifter picked us up. Our Chief Engineer, Charlie McLean of Helensburgh, and I managed to get into the same boat, half frozen. Ultimately, we landed in Margate. The first ship we saw was the *Duchess of Fife* so, of course we went on board. After some tea, we were directed to a survivor's centre. What a sight we looked! My trousers were ripped half way up the leg, and I had no cap or jacket. Charlie McLean was worse. He had no socks or shirt - nothing but a pair of trousers and a singlet. They gave me a raincoat three sizes too big, and Charlie McLean got a Khaki great-coat. We collected railway warrants and set off on survivor's leave.'

Back at Dunkirk, after the *Waverley's* gallant rescue attempt the *Eagle III* was still aground. 'As the tide went out so did our chances of getting off,' said Robert Lindsay. 'Candidly, we thought our number was up, when we were left high and dry on the sands. We advised the troops to transfer to other ships further down the beach, but many of the preferred to take the chance that we would get off. We were bombed and machine gunned, but some how we managed to survive. Then the tide came back. When we had sufficient water, we tried the engines. Eventually, at 6 in the evening, we got off after surviving 10 hours of bombing.'

The *Marmion* had an exciting third run through a lot of shelling.

She hadn't enough coal to make a fourth trip. The *Eagle III,* and the *Duchess of Fife* made more successful trips. They, too, were shelled on their last trips. Meanwhile, the 11th Flotilla - from Rothesay - lost their race. They were held up twice for coaling, and as they steamed into Dover, the last of the little ships was returning from Dunkirk. Casualties had so depleted the flotillas that a drastic re-organisation was necessary. The *Eagle III, Marmion* and *Duchess of Fife* went back to Harwich, to the 12th Flotilla. The fastest paddlers joined the 10th Flotilla and swept from the from The Downs to Beachy Head. That brought them right into the Battle of Britain. As the Nazis bombers returned from their missions, they dropped any spare bombs, and machine gunned the little ship operating round what was called 'Hell Fire Corner'. The *Kylemore,* veteran of the 10th Flotilla, fell a victim and sank in the Thames Estuary. Better armed ships were brought into the area and the *Jupiter, Juno, Jeanie Deans, Mercury* and *Caledonia* were transferred to Portland for sweeping operations. Yet gradually the Luftwaffe brought the entire South of England within its radius.

In one raid the ships' gunners brought down three of the enemy planes. The credit for two 'kills' went to the *Jupiter's* gun crews, although no claim was made on their behalf. As one of the crew remarked, with so many guns going, it was difficult to say whose shot registered the kill. Captain Archibald Campbell, of Greenock, was Navigating Officer of the *Mercury:* 'As the planes roared overhead, they plastered us and swept round in a circle and came back in again. Every time they came in, our guns opened up. Then they got us, right on the bows. The 12 pounder gun was destroyed and the entire gun crew of eight killed. The other ships got off lightly - practically untouched. The *Mercury* had to go to Weymouth for repairs. When we were made sea worthy again, the Flotilla was back on the Clyde. We followed them.'

The diesel electric powered *Talisman,* commissioned as the anti-aircraft vessel *Aristocrat,* had a busy war career including a role as HQ ship Arromanches during the Normandy landings *(IWM).*

Distinctive camouflage paint effectively breaks up the lines of the anti-aircraft vessel *HMS Goatfell,* otherwise the Clyde paddler *Caledonia,* previously used as a minesweeper *(IWM).*

When the paddlers steamed through the defence boom across the Clyde from the Cloch to Dunoon, the crews saw for the first time the transformation of the river. Ships of all sizes, from troop ships to barges, were being loaded and unloaded. Floating docks and cranes were in position. The Clyde Anchorages Emergency Port had been installed. As the Luftwaffe concentrated on London, Liverpool and Hull, the Clyde and its deep water fjord-like lochs was the natural selection as a safe anchorages to keep open the lifeline of Britain. The Clyde became the hub of military traffic. The gigantic troop movements needed brought in *Queen Mary* and the *Queen Elizabeth.* Again, the Clyde steamers played a prominent part. The first turbine steamer in the world, the *King Edward,* was ferrying men and materials to the waiting liners and with her were the *Duchess of Argyll* and the *Duchess of Hamilton.* They carried millions of Allied fighting men and enemy prisoners, out and in from the Tail o' the Bank.

Late in the summer of 1940, yet another of the pleasure steamers had been called to service - the *Talisman.* The only sea-going diesel electric drive paddle ship in the world, this pioneer went into commission as a Bofors-gun vessel, under the name *HMS Aristocrat.* She soon proved aptness of her peacetime nickname 'The Wasp.' And she had a sting! Repairs had now been completed to the 11th Flotilla ships and they set off for Milford Haven. Captain Campbell was again on the bridge of the *Mercury*: 'Late in 1940 we resumed minesweeping operations from Milford Haven. Our voyages often took us well into the Atlantic south of the Irish Coast. For three months we swept without loss. Then came Christmas Day, 1940. The *Mercury* had three Clyde steamers in the company that day - *Helvellyn, Scawfell* and *Goatfell,* better known as *Juno, Jupiter* and our sister vessel *Caledonia.* The *Jeanie Deans* was in dock for repairs after some heavy weather. We were about 50 miles from Milford Haven when we caught a mine in the sweep wire and it exploded under the stern. For a moment we thought the ship was doomed. She shuddered like a leaf. The stern plates were badly buckled, and we were making a lot of water. The flotilla stood by us. There was just a chance that the pumps could keep us afloat until we reached port and so we were taken in tow by one of the trawlers. For four hours, that trawler towed us through the stormy seas. Just off the Smalls, rocky islands off the Welsh coast, it was obvious the ship couldn't take it. The seas won the battle with the pumps and we began to settle. The order went out to abandon ship and we transferred to the trawler. We steamed around her to the last.'

Defeated in the Battle of Britain, the Luftwaffe settled down to the policy of terror raids. With London and the Thames the main objectives, specially converted Anti-Aircraft ships were assembled to form the Thames Local Defence Flotilla. Among the initial members was the *Talisman* and the 'Wasp' needed her sting. William Douglas of Helensburgh, was the chief engineer on board her: 'Our guns were in action every night, and almost every day, in the Thames. The Nazis bombed and dropped mines on us at all hours, and the *Talisman* had many narrow escapes. On one occasion seven ships were blown up inside a radius of a mile. Our crew had a hectic time lifesaving in the midst of these sinking vessels. We carried on for months before we were transferred to a quieter zone for a break. The *Royal Eagle,* a famous Thames paddler and the *Talisman* proceeded to Loch-na-Keil, north of Oban. But that was no rest cure for us. Preparations were being made for the landings in Algiers and most of the transports were being assembled in that neighbourhood. Our most thrilling experience there was during a gale. The giant Canadian Pacific liner *Empress of Canada* dragged her anchor and was blown ashore. The *Talisman* greatly helped in towing her off the beach. Eventually, sailed south again.'

Meanwhile a re-shuffle was taking place among the Clyde paddlers. The *Jupiter, Juno, Caledonia* and *Jeanie Deans* were withdrawn from minesweeping. They went to London for conversion as A/A ships. The *Eagle III* and the *Duchess of Fife*

The nearly new Caledonian Steam Packet paddler *Jupiter* went to war as *HMS Scawfell* and returned to see further service until 1957. Sister ship *Juno (HMS Helvellyn)* was not so lucky, falling victim to enemy bombing in London during 1941.

Jeanie Deans, long distance excursion steamer of the Craigendoran fleet in the 1930s, helped to defend London as an anti-aircraft vessel from 1941. Some 25 years later she returned to the Thames as *Queen of the South* but an ambitious attempt to revive steamer excursions in 1966 and 1967 was doomed to failure *(IWM)*.

The faithful *Marmion* sunk at Harwich following a bombing raid in April 1941. In the black and white of this picture, *Marmion's* funnel looks for all the world as if it is in the famous red, white and black of the LNER and previously North British fleet based at Craigendoran *(Rev. Wm. C. Galbraith collection).*

were transferred from Harwich to Hull. The *'Fife'* was later sent to the Forth and acted as a training ship in a School of Minesweeping. The gallant old *Duchess of Rothesay,* now nearing her jubilee, was transferred to Brightlingsea as an accommodation ship. April 1941 marked the end of yet another Clyde paddler. The *Marmion* this time, sank during a blitz on Harwich. Within a month the Luftwaffe claimed another Clyde steamer. Chief Engineer Benny Howe, of Greenock, was on board *Goatfell,* better known as the *Caledonia.* He recalled: 'The *Caledonia* and *Juno* were being re-fitted as A/A ships in Surrey Commercial Docks in London. Nearby, in the Royal Albert Docks, the *Jeanie Deans* and the *Jupiter* were on the same errand. The London Blitz was at its height during this time. We didn't get much sleep, I can tell you. By day, the welders and riveters were busy; by night and often by day, Jerry was over. Our off-duty hours were as busy as the working ones. Although the ship was in for re-armament, I was busy with an overhaul of the engines. I was down below in the engine room of the *Caledonia* the day the *Juno* was hit. She got a bomb right between her two funnels. the *Caledonia* lay just astern. Every member of our crew who could be spared went to help and they managed to rescue quite a few of the injured. Two of our ratings, William Snoddie and Jack Hulme, both from Greenock, were commended for bravery. The *Juno* was doomed, however. Her back was broken.

'Our re-armament was finished within ten weeks. Few people would have recognised us. Our decks literally bristled with guns. One 12 pounder forward, four two pounder pom-poms and six Oerlikons. A new radar room was installed in what had been the Captain's cabin. The *Caledonia, Jeanie Deans* and *Jupiter* were re-commissioned on 8th May, 1941, as anti-aircraft vessels. Next day, we all lay in dock awaiting the arrival of our naval ratings. We were all glad to be leaving London. But that night, Jerry came over again, and the *Caledonia* got it. A bomb dropped just off our port paddle box. Three ratings were killed and many injured. The ship suffered a lot from blast and repairs delayed our departure until the end of the month. Eventually, we joined the Thames Local Defence Flotilla.'

By the end of 1941, the ranks of the Clyde steamers had been reduced by five - *Juno, Kylemore, Mercury, Waverley* and the *Marmion*. More re-groupings of the rest of the fleet had to be made as the tide of war changed. The *Caledonia* and the *Jupiter* left the Thames to do the same job on the Humber; the *Eagle III* was joined by her pre-war companion, the *Queen Empress*. The *Talisman* went south again, and joined the *Jeanie Deans* in the Thames Local Defence Flotilla. That year, 1942, there were more rumours that something big was afoot. When *Talisman* was ordered to Sheerness for 'special duties' these rumours ran riot among the crew. Complete with load of medical supplies and medical staff, the *Talisman* left Sheerness on its mystery mission. She steamed into the English Channel before the crew knew they were bound for Portsmouth. There, they took on four hundred Canadians. Once again they steamed off. Night after night, the *Talisman* made this hush-hush journey from Portsmouth to the Dorset coast. The Commandos disembarked and made a raiding foray inland. They returned to the ship to go back to Portsmouth. Just as the crew were getting accustomed to the routine, orders were received to proceed to Newhaven. There, a surprise awaited them. The crew was confined to the ship. They were told they were going to take part in the first landing on the continent of Europe. The trips from Portsmouth to the Dorset coast had been the actual steaming distance of the raiding mission. Their job was to take the troops as near the beach as possible. On the return journey, they were to look after the casualties. And if the ship were sunk, the crew had to make their way into the interior of France and try to contact the underground organisation. Security officials took away all log books and all personal belongings and means of identification from the crew. They were advised to write a letter to their next of kin.

But it wasn't until the fifth night they got sailing orders - back to Sheerness. Months later, they heard about the Dieppe raid - the raid they almost took part in. During the next two years, the *Jupiter* and the *Caledonia* became utility vessels. After their spell in the Humber, they went south to Harwich. There, they escorted Trinity House vessels employed in buoying new channels. A few months of this routine and then off again. Herbert Branford, a Yorkshireman domiciled in Greenock was the chief engineer on the *Jupiter*: 'Under the wartime name of *HMS Scawfell*, the *Jupiter* was a lucky ship. Although we had many exciting trips and experiences, there was only one incident recorded on board. That was when an incendiary bomb struck us. I was working near the store-room at the time when it came sputtering down the companionway. Within a couple of minutes, I had that bomb out! Up on deck, the watch reported all clear and most of the crew knew nothing of that raid until they rose next morning. We hoped our luck would hold when we heard of our next detail. Based on North Shields, we became the 'Moonlight Patrol'. We steamed out and collected our charges, to shepherd them through 'E-boat alley' each night for the next 12 months. Then came a change. We received orders to proceed to the Solent. We had a good idea that we were going to take part in the much talked of 'D-Day'. In the Solent, the *Jupiter* and the *Caledonia* were separated for the first time in six years. We were loaded with ammunition, fuel and stores and the *Caledonia* went off to Weymouth. We lay off the Isle of Wight awaiting orders.'

Preparations for the invasion of Europe had been going on all along the South Coast. Secretly, sections of a gigantic sea harbour - the unprecedented 'Mulberry' - were being collected at strategic

points. Rehearsals for the landings all along the coast. One of the A/A ships protecting the pontoon dock convoys was the *Talisman*. It was no surprise to her crew when they were made headquarters ship for Mulberry Harbour. On D-Day, the *Talisman* sailed for France. Chief Engineer William Douglas, vividly recalled being the vanguard of the invasion: 'We had really little time to think of the task ahead. We were busy checking up last minute details. However, as the technical staff of the harbour and the various Army officials came on board, we all asked the same questions. Is everything ready? Will everything go all right? What kind of reception will we get the other side? That night, the convoy, a huge crocodile of six ships abreast, steamed into the Channel bound for the Normandy coast. As the *Talisman* moved away from her parent ship, *HMS Despatch,* we got just the encouragement we needed. The ship's Electrical Officer, Alex Mitchell brought his bagpipes on deck and played us off. The *Talisman* arrived at Arromanches at half past four in the morning. The initial landings had been a success but we could hear the sound of battle inland, as we anchored a quarter of a mile from the shore. We had really little excitement. There was a little enemy air activity but nothing to speak of. Mostly, scattered raids were made by a few planes during the night. At 2 am on D-Day plus one, the Royal Engineers blew the first charge in the sea wall at Arromanches. Telephones were soon laid from ship to shore and a start was made in the building of the harbour. The first block ship, the *Alanbank,* was sunk at 5 pm. Gradually the harbour took shape. Phoenix pontoon docks were placed in position.

Opposite page: *Caledonia,* as *HMS Goatfell,* pictured at Immingham towards the end of her minesweeping days and still carrying the pennant number J125. Back in Clyde service until 1961, *Caledonia* was later established as a floating pub and restaurant moored on the Thames in Central London until gutted by fire in 1979. *(Clyde River Steamer Club).*

Bombardons, to save the harbour from the heavy seas, were put into place and *Talisman* was detailed to direct the incoming ships to the various beaches.'

On D-Day plus one, the *Jupiter* left the Solent. She had on board the 128th US Task Force. After discharging her complement on the beaches at Normandy, she was assigned as an A/A ship protecting Mulberry, but only one ship was sunk by air attack during the first three days. On D-Day plus five, the *Caledonia* left Weymouth. She was assigned to act as communications between signal station and incoming traffic and act as an A/A ship when necessary. She met the *Jupiter* again at Omaha Beach. The work of supplying the liberating armies went smoothly for the first few days. Then a heavy wind sprang up; soon it had increased to a gale. The *Caledonia* was ordered to return to the Solent for shelter. The *Jupiter* remained. The man in charge of the engine room was Herbert Branford: 'Many ships were blown ashore by that gale, and the Harbour was rendered useless for the job intended. The *Jupiter* went inside the harbour for shelter. More ships went ashore and more than once we touched bottom ourselves. It was finally decided that we would be safer at sea and we were ordered out in the full fury of the gale. Seas like mountains lashed over our bows. As the storm continued, our fuel and water started to run short. Drinking water was rationed on the third day out. At the end of the fourth day, each man was allowed one pint per day. Coal was becoming a serious problem. Normally *Jupiter* consumed one ton of coal per hour at a speed of 12 knots. On the fifth day, there was barely one ton of coal in our bunkers. But the weather improved, and we were just able steam back to the Mulberry Harbour.'

The *Talisman* had to leave French waters for bow damage to be repaired after a collision with barges. Instead of going back to Mulberry as expected, the ship was ordered to proceed to Harwich.

The largest Thames paddler *Royal Eagle* bristling with weaponry as an anti-aircraft ship. It was responsible for transporting 2,657 men home from Dunkirk and returned to excursions in 1946, but was withdrawn after a short season in 1950, completing only a modest 13 summers of sailings from Tower Pier to Thames Estuary resorts *(IWM)*.

They steamed along the coast and were just leaving the English Channel when coming under fire from German shore batteries at Cap Gris Nez. Two crew members were wounded as six shrapnel hits were received and *Talisman's* first weeks at Harwich were spent under repair. As the war in Europe entered its final phase the desperate Nazi's unleased a new horror, the V1 flying bomb and

crews of the paddle minesweepers had their first experience of them when Portsmouth was targeted from launch sites in Northern France. Bob Howe, remembered his ship's first encounter: "Every gun in the vicinity opened up on the V.1 None of us hit it, though. We had five more that night. Next day our flotilla was ordered to stand by as defence ships. The six of us the *Glen Usk, Glen Avon,*

Jupiter, Sandown, Ryde and the *Caledonia* all pre-war pleasure steamers, took up strategic positions in a line from Southsea to the Isle of Wight. Within two months the Army threw Germans out of the launching sites and V.1's had petered out in the Portsmouth area. But London wasn't so lucky.'

London certainly wasn't. Just after D-Day, a young Paisley man, leading Signaller Robert Millar was told to report to the *Jeanie Deans*: 'At first, I hardly recognised the old Clyde favourite in her camouflage paint. Among the crew of 75, there were six or seven Scotsman and I soon settled down. Life on the paddler was much different from a destroyer. There wasn't so much excitement, but I had better quarters. Our job was to proceed to a given position in the Thames Estuary for V.1. patrols and lookout for mine-laying aircraft. The gun crews brought down three V.1's and several aircraft. As we were at sea four days out of every five, we had some hectic times. But we also had lighter moments. One of the Flotilla was the Thames paddler, the *Royal Eagle*. Her crew claimed she was the fastest paddle steamer in the world. Then one day we put the claim of speed to the test. Out in the Thames went the oil-burning *Royal Eagle* and the coal fired *Jeanie Deans* raced to our positions. It must have looked as if the *'Jeanie'* was lying a smoke screen. But if the claim of the *Royal Eagle's* crew had been correct, after that day it was no longer true. The *'Jeanie'* won. And I was there when it happened!'

As the Allied Armies swept along the seaboard of Europe, the little ships were bringing supplies to the liberated ports. The *Talisman* left Harwich on the first convoy to Antwerp, and the *Jupiter* and the *Caledonia* followed her within a few days. There they had the job of minespotting and directing all incoming traffic. The next priority in shipping during that eventful summer of 1945 was the provision of food supplies for the starving population of Europe. The *Eagle III* and the *Queen Empress* were employed on this mercy mission and made several trips to the Dutch coast. Prominent on the hull of the *Queen Empress* were paintings of two planes to denote her aircraft kills during her stay in the Humber. The Nazis tried every trick to hold back the Allies from the Dutch ports. As their depleted Air Force was swept from the skies, they hurled large numbers of rocket projectiles on the occupied harbours. Chief Engineer Howe was with the *Caledonia* on the Scheldt: 'Our stay in the Dutch ports was worst than the London blitz. What a bombardment. The Nazis sent over V.1's every ten minutes. Then they let loose something new. It was our first introduction to V.2's. During the day, we could see the huge smoke trails of the rocket soaring high in the sky. At night they were streaks of fire rising into the stratosphere. If you heard them explode, you were safe. Nobody heard the one that got him. We were glad to be released from duty on the Scheldt. We returned to the Clyde on VE Day plus one.'

The *Jupiter* led the way back to the Clyde for the pleasure steamers. During her six year war service, she destroyed three aircraft and was credited with several probable hits. Into the refitting yard she went for complete overhaul and reconditioning. The crew's quarters, with pin-ups over the beds were transformed into luxurious lounges again. She re-appeared in her former bright company colours and, after her trials, took up the Holy Loch run in February, 1946. The *Caledonia, Duchess of Fife* and the *Duchess of Hamilton* were reconditioned in time to take up the steamer service in June. The first LNER steamer to resume was the *Jeanie Deans*. A month later, in July, the *Talisman* re-appeared and then the LNER perpetuated the name *Waverley* on the new paddle steamer, launched on 2nd October 1946 from the yard of A & J Inglis, Pointhouse, Glasgow and, fittingly, Captain Cameron was its first Skipper!

One Officer's camera tells the evacuation story...

Some of the most remarkable pictures of the Dunkirk evacuation, including poignant images familiar in just about every corner of the world during the last half a century, were taken by John Rutherford Crosby, son of a Glasgow bookseller and a Sub Lieutenant aboard *HMS Oriole,* the paddle steamer better known from the Clyde of his boyhood as the *Eagle III* of the Williamson Buchanan fleet. An avid photographer, Crosby, always known by his second christian name, took his camera to war and these pages include some of the shots taken during the *Oriole's* first visit to the little resort of La Panne, a few miles east of Dunkirk and close to the Belgian border. With the steamer high and dry after being deliberately beached to

Left: Rutherford Crosby on the beach at La Panne with the grounded *Oriole* in the background. Above: the beach scene with *Oriole* (far left) aground with vessels off shore including Dutch motor coasters, two Royal Navy destroyers and, to the right, the paddle minesweeper *Waverley,* sunk later in the day.

aid the evacuation, Crosby was able to walk across the sand and into the town. Later, as the tide turned, it was back to the *Oriole* as men waded out up to their necks in the water to board. Crosby, seen on the right with rifle slung over his shoulder, tin hat at the ready, and the beached *Oriole* behind, had little time for pictures as loading got underway but, back at Harwich, his precious film was eagerly seized by a journalist and the pictures appeared in newspapers and magazines far and wide. The *Oriole* returned, again to the beaches near La Panne and, for a second time, was driven ashore, to load before returning to land troops in Margate. Twice more the *Oriole's* antiquated single diagonal engine powered the vessel back across the Channel, on these occasions to load men from Dunkirk itself. Then Crosby and all the remainder of the exhausted officers and crew were relieved by the crew of the *Plinlimmon* (Campbell's *Cambria)* and *Oriole* made a fifth return trip. *Oriole* was officially recorded as landing 2,587 men but this took no account of hundreds more who crossed the steamer's decks to reach other vessels. Crosby remained with minesweepers as the war continued but lost his life in 1943 when the *Horatio* was sunk off the African coast near Bizerta. These pictures were made available to Russell Plummer for his 1990 book *'The Ships That Saved An Army'* by John Crosby, Rutherford's son.

The beach at La Panne from the deck of the *Oriole* and, below, just after as two German bombs explode simultaneously. Below left is another shot of the *Oriole* high and dry with a feather of steam from behind the funnel as the safety valves lift.

Troops wait in an orderly line to be hauled aboard the *Oriole* - perhaps the most famous Dunkirk evacuation picture of them all.
Above, some of the rescued troops line the rails as the paddler heads back to Harwich, others sleep where they sit on deck.

Three views by Rutherford Crosby of the Clyde steamer *Eagle III*
which he joined at the end of 1939 in the much altered guise of the paddle minesweeper *Oriole*.

The Campbell steamer *Glen Avon* heading away from Dunkirk with some of the 900 men returned home during 'Operation Dynamo.'
A number of the troops have even managed to find space on the peace time reserved deck above the after shelter *(A.G.Taylor).*

Approximately half the paddle vessels requisitioned for Naval service and pressed into use as minesweepers or anti-aircraft vessels, took part in 'Operation Dynamo,' the evacuation of the British Expeditionary Force from the harbour at Dunkirk and beaches running east from the town to the Belgian border. It is an event that crops up repeatedly in this book during some of the individual accounts of Second World War service with paddle steamers, in the course of illustrations and the listings of the ships themselves.

OPERATION DYNAMO

The story of the amazing nine day operation that succeeded during the nine days from 27th May to 4th June 1940 in returning a total of 338,226 men to British shores, has been told on many occasions and in far greater depth than is possible in a volume as modest as this one. We confine ourselves to personal recollections and pictures, but do offer a brief account of the contribution of individual paddle vessels, two of them called directly from Isle of Wight ferry services and sent across without armament and time for only primitive efforts to camouflage their still largely peacetime colours.

More than half a century on, two of the steamers which took part in the evacuation, the *Medway Queen* and *Princess Elizabeth*, are still in existence. *Medway Queen* completed a remarkable seven trips to the beaches or Dunkirk Harbour and is officially credited with bringing home 3,056 men, although this figure was always regarded as a chronic underestimate by officers and crew members. The 316 ton steamer was even reported sunk at one stage of the evacuation, the crew hearing a BBC radio report of their demise while making one of the last trips back. The following day the Admiralty issued a statement: 'The paddle minesweeper *Medway Queen*, believed lost, has now arrived safely in port!'

Both *Medway Queen* and the *Princess Elizabeth* returned to

THE DUNKIRK EVACUATION 27TH MAY - 4TH JUNE 1940

peace time service until the 1960s and were each subsequently opened in static roles, *Medway Queen* at Binfield on the River Medina between Cowes and Newport from 1966, and *Princess Elizabeth* on the Thames in Central London between 1970 and 1987. *Medway Queen* became little more than a sunken wreck but was moved back to the River Medway on a submersible barge in 1984 with restoration work beginning in earnest three years later. It has continued to a stage where an operational business plan for the vessel was announced in April this year.

Princess Elizabeth was later acquired for a static role on the River Seine near the centre of Paris and opened as an arts and conference centre in 1991.

Officially 23 paddle steamers participated in 'Operation Dynamo,' with four further steamers also widely regarded as having played some part in the evacuation.

Here is a summary of the steamers that went to Dunkirk, six of them never to return:

The last few crew members prepare to abandon the *Brighton Belle* from the bow as the little paddler settles by the stern on 28th May 1940 after running over the submerged wreck during a return crossing from Dunkirk carrying an estimated 800 men. All the troops and crew were taken off by other vessels including the paddler *Medway Queen* (IWM).

BRIGHTON BELLE
Crossed from Dover with other ships of the 10th Flotilla on 27th May, loaded 800 troops and while under air attack during return voyage ran over the submerged wreck near the North Goodwins. As *Brighton Belle* settled by the stern all troops, crew - and the captain's dog - were taken off by the *Medway Queen*.

BRIGHTON QUEEN
Ordered south from the Forth, *Brighton Queen* refuelled at Harwich and then went to Bray Beach and used her own boats to load over 100 troops. The steamer also towed a disabled Dutch coaster until its crew managed to re-start the engine. *Brighton Belle* landed her troops at Margate and returned to berth in Dunkirk Harbour taking on 600 French and Algerians. Twenty minutes after leaving the vessel suffered a direct hit and had to be abandoned.
Official record: 160 men landed.

CRESTED EAGLE
Recalled to Sheerness from patrol in Thames Estuary on 25th May and sent to La Panne on the 28th. Moving on to Dunkirk Harbour, the paddler succeeded in berthing outside the East Mole, taking on a full complement of men, including survivors from the Isle of Man Steam Packet Company's *Fenella*. Off Malo-le-Bains *Crested Eagle* came under sustained aerial attack and was hit aft of the bridge. Two more bombs ignited fuel tanks and the after part of the vessel became a blazing inferno. Although the minesweeper *Albury* picked up survivors, many lives were lost

DEVONIA
Sister ship of *Brighton Queen* and also a member of the 7th Flotilla. Crossed from Harwich to La Panne on 30th May and used own boat to ferry men from beach. Came under air attack during which an explosion close to the stern caused leaks. Orders given for the steamer to be beached and abandoned inshore for use as a boarding point by the troops. Crew transferred to Dutch coaster *Hilda* and then to destroyer *Scimitar*.

DUCHESS OF FIFE
Part of the 12th Flotilla from Harwich, *Duchess of Fife* first crossed to La Panne on 28th May, loading troops from small boats and taking them to

Margate. Two further crossings were completed, including one to Dunkirk itself. **Official record: 1,801 men landed.**

EMPEROR OF INDIA
Fitted out at Southampton and sent to Dover to join 10th Flotilla. Set off on possibly only crossing to Dunkirk on 27th May, returning to Dover. Later used as anti-aircraft ship and then as a training vessel for stokers. **Official record: 642 men landed.**

ESSEX QUEEN
Reported in the Dover area before the evacuation and according to the log of the *Princess Elizabeth,* small boats used to load troops from the beach at La Panne we handed over to the *Essex Queen.* The steamer's name does not appear in any official records, however. Later *Essex Queen* was used as a hospital ship to assist in relief work after air raids in London's docklands.

FRESHWATER
Another vessel not officially listed at Dunkirk but subject of well documented reports that actor and peacetime yachtsman Moran Caplat joined the ship at Sheerness to take part in the evacuation. *Freshwater* returned to continue war service as an examination vessel at Portland and later Portsmouth.

GLEN AVON
One of the Campbell paddlers in the 8th Flotilla sent south from North Shields, *Glen Avon* completed at least two crossings to load troops from the beaches near La Panne. Converted to anti-aircraft vessel it had a communications role during the Normandy Landings. Later in 1944, *Glen Avon* foundered in a storm when caught at anchor off French coast. **Official record: 888 men landed.**

GLEN GOWER
Also from the 8th Flotilla, *Glen Gower* completed three trips. During one, loaded with over 500 men, the steamer grounded near La Panne but was towed off by another Campbell paddler *Snaefell,* the Bristol Channel

Two views of the *Devonia* abandoned on the beach at La Panne in June 1940, both from German sources, and with soldiers posing in front of the vessel in the lower view. Widespread reports that *Devonia* had been salvaged and taken to Germany for river service were never found to have any foundation *(Richard Howarth collection).*

The Campbell fleet was represented in the Dunkirk evacuation by eight steamers, three of which failed to return.
Top: *Glenmore,* following conversion to an anti-aircraft ship.
Above: *Glen Avon,* a Dunkirk survivor but later lost in severe weather off the French Coast.
Below: *Glen Gower* is seen off the French coast with decks crowded with troops *(Richard Howarth collection).*

was then allowed to become almost derelict before restoration started.
Official record: 3,064 men landed

ORIOLE
The Dun*Waverley,* as both were attacked from the air. Renamed *Glenmore* after conversion to anti-aircraft vessel in 1941, it finished the war in the Scheldt Estuary.
Official record: 1,235 men landed.

GOLDEN EAGLE
Fitted for anti-aircraft duties, *Golden Eagle* sailed from Sheerness on 29th May on the first of three crossings, picking-up survivors from the Clyde steamer *Waverley.* Another trip to Bray Beach and then Dunkirk itself produced a loading in excess of a thousand men. Returning from a last visit to Dunkirk Harbour on 2nd June, *Golden Eagle* had to reduce speed after a rope became entangled in the port paddle wheel.
Official record: 1,751 men landed.

GRACIE FIELDS
Set off with the 10th Flotilla on 27th May and returned safely to land troops in Dover. Some 750 men were taken on board in a second visit to th° beaches but vessel was bombed near Middel Kirk Buoy and began sinking despite attempts by the sloop *Pangbourne* to effect a tow.
Official record: 281 men landed.

LAGUNA BELLE
No mention of this veteran is made in official lists although it is reported to have set sail with other ships from the 10th Flotilla on 27th May. Converted to anti-aircraft vessel and finished the war as an accommodation ship.

MARMION
Sailed from a base at Harwich direct to Dunkirk with other paddle minesweepers of the 12th Flotilla. More details are included in the chapter dealing with the Scottish paddlers. The vessel was sunk by bombing at Harwich in 1941 and, although raised, was later declared a total loss.
Official record: 713 men landed.

the Isle of Wight in 1966 by the late 'Jack' Graves, her First Lieutenant at Dunkirk, it was then allowed to become almost derelict before restoration started.
Official record: 3,064 men landed

ORIOLE

The Dunkirk contribution of this Clyde veteran, powered by an antiquated single diagonal engine, is one of the most fully documented of any participating vessel. Five trips were completed with the entire crew being replaced for the last crossing by that from the paddle minesweeper *Plinlimmon*. Later used as accommodation ship and finally laid-up in Holy Loch.
Official record: 2,587 troops landed.

PLINLIMMON

After years of doubts it has been confirmed that the Campbell paddler, part of the 7th Flotilla, completed one trip, landing troops at Margate, before being barred from further crossings because of defective degaussing equipment. However, *Plinlimmon's* crew relieved that of *Oriole* on 3rd of June and made one more crossing.
Official record: 900 troops landed.

PRINCESS ELIZABETH

Came relatively un scathed through four return trips to beaches east of Dunkirk, first crossing with the rest of the 10th Flotilla to La Panne on 27th May and thereafter operating independently, once back to La Panne and twice to Bray. Finished service as anti-aircraft ship in 1944.
Official record: 1,673 men landed.

Medway Queen in Ramsgate Harbour early in 1940, shortly before making seven trips to Dunkirk to return over 3,000 men. While most of the coal burning paddlers had to drop out of the evacuation because of re-fuelling problems, the oil burning *Medway Queen* sailed on into history
(J.D.Graves).

PORTSDOWN

Taken off the Ryde ferry and commissioned at Sheerness on 1st June. Classed as a personnel ship, *Portsdown* crossed unarmed and used own boats to load men, later being held bow on to the beach. Assisted other vessels returning to Ramsgate. Resumed Isle of Wight sailings until mined and sunk in Spithead September 1941.
Official record: 618 men landed.

QUEEN OF THANET

The Senior Officer's ship of the 7th Minesweeping Flotilla made four trips, mainly to Dunkirk Harbour, returning to Margate, and also distinguished herself when taking large numbers off the damaged personnel ship *Prague* on 1st June. Also played a major role prior, during and after the Normandy Landings in 1944.
Official record: 2,500 men landed.

ROYAL EAGLE

An anti-aircraft vessel from the Thames Flotilla, *Royal Eagle* was the largest paddler present at Dunkirk and came under air attack on 43 occasions while making three return crossings, first sailing to Ramsgate and then landing more than a thousand men, including seriously wounded, at its Sheerness base on 31st May. Resumed Thames patrols for the remainder of the war.
Official record: 2,657 men landed.

Left: The *Queen of Thanet,* converted for passenger use after being built as a First World War paddle minesweeper, was minesweeping again before the end of 1939, and went on to distinguish herself at Dunkirk and at the Normandy Landings. In the top picture of the entrance to Dunkirk Harbour at the height of the evacuation, the twin-funnelled *Queen of Thanet* can be seen on the extreme right, approaching with West Mole. (IWM) The other pictures are from the collection of Ken Jenkins, son of a pre-war director of P & A Campbell, show (left) the *Skiddaw (Britannia)* and *Plinlimmon (Cambria)* astern after a North Sea sweep, while (right) the same decks are crowded with troops as the *Queen of Thanet* returns from Dunkirk on 1st June 1940, having taken on as many as 2,000 men from the sinking personnel ship *Prague*.

SANDOWN

As Senior Officer's vessel, *Sandown* led the 10th Flotilla to Dunkirk on 27th May and again next day, subsequently sailing independently. While returning to France on 1st June the *Sandown* used its motor boat to take 250 men off a grounded drifter. Re-armed for anti-aircraft duties, *Sandown* supported the Normandy Landings and was finally used on the Scheldt.
Official record: 1,861 men landed

SNAEFELL

Sailed south with other Campbell steamers in the 8th Flotilla, crossing with *Glen Avon* and *Glen Gower,* succeeding in hauling the latter into deep water after it went aground. Continued minesweeping until sunk off the Tyne 13 months later.
Official record: 981 men landed.

THAMES QUEEN

Another vessel popularly believed to have been involved in at least the early stages of the evacuation despite the lack of any references in the official records. *Thames Queen* was certainly at Dover before the start of 'Operation Dynamo' and is claimed to have sailed as part of the 10th Flotilla on 27th May.

WAVERLEY

After taking in stores and fuel at Great Yarmouth, *Waverley* received orders to Dunkirk from an MTB in the Thames Estuary. Arriving off La Panne on 29th May the vessel loaded an estimated 600 men under air attack and was heading for home when struck by three bombs in quick succession and had to be abandoned.

WESTWARD HO

By the time *Westward Ho* arrived from the Forth the evacuation was well underway. The steamer made two crossings and possibly a third, troops landed at Margate including one large French contingent. *Westward Ho* resumed minesweeping until boiler trouble resulted it in being used as an accommodation ship at Dartford.
Official record: 1,686 men landed.

HMS Snaefell, the Campbell *Waverley,* heading for beaches east of Dunkirk, towing small boats used for ferrying troops *(A.G.Taylor).*

WHIPPINGHAM

Taken off the Isle of Wight ferry and commissioned as a personnel vessel at Sheerness. Made one crossing but succeeded in loading 2,700 men, more than twice its peacetime complement. The sponsons were less than a foot above the sea and the skipper described the vessel as being 'very much over loaded.' After resuming ferry duties *Whippingham* was requisitioned as a minesweeper in 1941 and later converted to anti-aircraft vessel.
Official record: 2,700 men landed.

KINGSWEAR CASTLE'S WAR ROLE

The superbly restored Kingswear Castle,now based on the River Medway, played its part towards the end of the Second World War. Built in 1924, yet powered by an engine completed 20 years earlier, Kingwear Castle and the rest of the River Dart Steamboat fleet were laid up immediately war was declared. It occasionally relieved on the Dartsmouth - Kingswear ferry and in 1941 sometimes stood in when the Totnes Castle provided a limited summer service. Kingwear Castle later acted as a stores vessel at Dittisham Pier and then, in the build-up to the Normandy Landings in 1944, was loaned to the United States Navy to serve as a tender in Dartmouth Harbour.

Exhausted soldiers, many sleeping where they sit, on the way home from Dunkirk aboard a Campbell paddler, thought to be the *Glen Avon* *(Courtesy Terry Sylvester)*.

SWEEPING WITH THE DEVONIA

Three views taken aboard the *Devonia* early in 1940. The open bridge of excursion sailings has been replaced by a wheelhouse with a canvas shrouded observation platform on top; the centre view shows the paddler's after decks with the sweeps out and, on the right, the First Lieutenant Charles Cox checks the sights of one of the Lewis guns.

WITH THE DEVONIA BEFORE DUNKIRK

Story and pictures
by Leslie Rashleigh

It was on New Year's Day 1940 and as a very inadequate RNVR signalman that I joined my first ship, the paddle minesweeper *Devonia* at West Hartlepool. She was on passage to the Firth of Forth following conversion at Milford Haven to operate as an Oropesa Minesweeper and with an armament consisting of one 12 pounder gun forward and Lewis gun mountings on each paddle sponson.

The complement consisted of Captain (a retired paddler skipper with the rank of Lieut. Commander, RNR), First Lieutenant (RNR), Sub. Lieut. (RNVR), Chief Engineer (Lieut. RNR), Second Engineer (Sub. Lieut. RNR), Coxswain (Petty Officer pensioner), Buffer (PO), one Leading Hand (RN), one leading hand (RNR), three Able Seamen (all RN) plus five Hull and three Stornoway fishermen. In addition there were 12 Maltese from Cardiff for engine room and stokehold duties, a cook (PO), steward (PO), telegraphist (RNVWR) and a signalman (RNVR).

When it came to accommodation, the Wardroom was aft and all other personnel, forward. Below the foredeck were two messes separated by a gangway to the paint and rope store. All the Maltese were in the port side mess and the seamen to starboard, while below on the lower deck were the POs and leading hands, plus additional sleeping accommodation for the seamen's mess. The telegraphist lived in comparative luxury having a bunk in the wireless cabin on the upper deck. The mess decks were very basic and heated by a round cast iron stove - with a stove pipe piercing the foredeck which

Just as during the 1914-1918 war, steamers from the Bristol fleet of P & A. Campbell were soon called- up,some within a few days of the start of the Second World War in September 1939. A dozen Campbell vessels flew the white ensign, most of them operating initially as minesweepers and here are accounts of service on two of then, the *Devonia* which retained her own name and *Britannia*, commissioned as *HMS Skiddaw*.

leaked in the early days until properly caulked! We were on canteen messing but the Maltese maintained a separate scheme with their own unofficial cook - who always seemed more competent than the ship's official cook!

Life on board was quite monotonous. We were in harbour at Granton most nights which was fortunate as on the few occasions were forced to anchor outside we usually found the odd mine floating nearby having broken adrift from our own field. We swept daily following a regular routine and usually paired with *Devonia's* sister ship *Brighton Queen*. After leaving harbour and passing through the boom defence from Inchkeith Island to the north shore of the Forth, we proceeded to just off Methil, a rendezvous point for convoys. There we streamed sweeps and followed the shipping channel. Sometimes the *Brighton Queen* would break off and proceed north of May Island but *Devonia* always took the southern channel past Bass Rock and towards St. Abbs Head before 'in sweeps' and home. On a couple of occasions we continued further and anchored for the night inside the Farne Islands.

Normally we returned to Granton and in view of the tricky and tiny harbour entrance, the captain was always anxious to get back while it was still light. This called for full speed which, in *Devonia's* case was considerable. Generally we returned independently and must have made an impressive sight our two funnels giving forth vast clouds of black smoke and tongues of flame. The heat inside the funnels was intense and with paint bubbling like lava, passing them meant hugging the ship's rails to avoid being scorched. The only time I tried the stokehold, I got no further than easing open the air lock door before being driven back by the heat from below. There was ample shore leave but Granton was rather dreary and appreciated mainly by the 'beer hounds' and party chasers. However, the occasional ride into Edinburgh was quite a change. Boiler cleaning leave was a welcome relief for all and usually lasted four days.

But in my time on board we never swept a single mine, not even

in our 'own' mine field, the *Devonia's* cutters for some reason seeming inadequate. One day in May 1940, after sweeping and while anchored for the night near the Farne Islands a signal was received ordering us to Tynemouth, Harwich and finally to Dunkirk. By the time we reached the swept channel across to France there was considerable two-way traffic and in addition to tugs towing long strings of motor cruisers and launches.

There was a lot of air activity, mainly bombing, and the Germans were also in Nieuport, in sight of the beaches, which they shelled spasmodically. We manned the 12 pounder and popped off a few shells and also used the Lewis guns, which helped morale if nothing else. We launched our boat to make a couple of runs to inshore, off-loading on to the *Hilda,* a small, one hold, high poop Dutch coaster manned by a Royal Navy Lieutenant with three ratings. Before long the bombing and shelling came too close for comfort and then we reeled from a stick of bombs immediately astern. This opened up *Devonia's* stern and before long the Commodore appeared to see the Captain. Because of the severity of the damage we were instructed to beach as far in as possible in the hope that the ship would act as a jetty for the troops - although at that time we were still too far out for the soldiers to wade.

When the order came to abandon ship the Buffer passed among us with the rum jar and everyone was told to take a stiff tot in case we ended up in the sea. After we beached I took the ship's confidential books and papers to the stokehold to be burnt and only the second engineer remained to assist, and then open the sea cocks. We left *Devonia* - and her unfinished day trip to France - in style and rowed across to the *Hilda.*

Left: *Devonia* at Milford Haven after being commissioned as a minesweeper in December 1940.

SPEEDING HOME ON THE BRITANNIA

by Hugh Drake

Following minesweeping training at *HMS Lochinvar,* we green Sub. Lieutenants (acting temporarily, probationary - and almost unpaid!) were drafted to Oropesa paddle minesweepers working from Granton and after previous experience with a drifter and an Admiralty Tree Class trawler, the main deck of these vessels seemed as large as a football field. I joined *HMS Skiddaw,* the former P & A.Campbell excursion vessel *Britannia,* dating from 1896 and which had also seen First World War service. The flotilla also included *HMS Plinlimmon, Britannia's* sister ship *Cambria.*

To my recollection they had no obstructions on the centre line bar the bridge and funnel, and my cabin, that of the second engineer in peace time, seemed as big as our dining room is now. I think they must have been the most luxurious quarters ever experienced by a young sub! We spent only a few weeks on these lovely old ships, much to my chagrin, as I had many trips on the Eagle Steamers from Tower Pier to Southend and Ramsgate in the late 1920s and 1930s and found that my fascination for their lovely engines had not waned and spent many off-duty hours in the engine room,

just as in peace time.

I particularly recall the speed of *Skiddaw* on the way home to base with as much as 17 knots achieved, especially if the Chief Engineer had a date! The funnel top glowed and paint blistered as we thundered our way back to Granton and entered the harbour going at least three-quarter speed to negotiate the tricky starboard bend to our berth. The Commander Minesweepers could not get used to a ship approaching at 14 knots or thereabouts only to have the skipper - a former paddle steamer master - to ring down 'stop' and 'full astern' to bring the ship alongside just where it should be. One other experience akin to the old film 'Tug Boat Annie' occurred when it became necessary for instant repairs to our vertical haystack boiler. Once fire was drawn and the Chief Engineer, enveloped in well soaked sacks and with a hose playing on him, crawled into the furnace to effect repairs. These boilers were fascinating with a domed top rising above the boat deck like an iron mole hill. In all a case of grand little ships doing a grand job! *(Picture: IWM)*

Although still carrying her minesweeping pennant number, the picture probably dates from 1942 when the *Cambria,* as *HMS Plinlimmon,*
visited the Thames for conversion to anti-aircraft vessel. As in sister ship *Britannia (HMS Skiddaw),*
the foremast has been moved aft to a position immediately in front of the bridge *(Richard Howarth collection).*

CAMPBELL FLYER **WAS** AT DUNKIRK!

Down the years, maritime historians have sought with varying degrees of success to establish whether particular vessels participated in 'Operation Dynamo', the evacuation of the British Expeditionary Force from Dunkirk in late May and the opening days of June 1940. Long a cause for debate was the presence of *HMS Plinlimmon,* the paddle minesweeper better known as *Cambria* and one of the fliers in the Campbell fleet and a vessel which once held claims to being Britain's fastest excursion steamer. It has since been proved conclusively that not only was *Plinlimmon* there in her own right, the crew also volunteered as a man to make a subsequent crossing aboard another paddler, *HMS Oriole,* the Clyde stalwart *Eagle III!*

It is perhaps this change of crews that has led to the confusion, but *Plinlimmon,* a member of the 7th Minesweeping Flotilla, based at Granton, was amongst a number of paddlers ordered south, arriving in Harwich from where it set out for the French coast at 0455hrs on 31st May, under the command of Lieut. G.P.Baker, RNVR. It arrived off La Panne at 1225hrs and took on 30 troops from a disabled motor boat before moving on to Dunkirk and was secured alongside the East Pier to embark around 900 troops.

Plinlimmon left at 1740 and 15 minutes later stopped to pick up a downed Royal Air Force pilot from the sea. It arrived in Margate at 2100 in the evening but after unloading was debarred from making a second crossing as the vessel's degaussing equipment as protection against magnetic mines was defective. Then, on 3rd June, when the former Williamson-Buchanan veteran *Oriole* reached Margate after a fourth crossing to Dunkirk, her exhausted crew was replaced

Confirmation of the Cambria's rolé during 'Operation Dynamo' is provided by Russell Plummer

by that of the *Plinlimmon.* After unloading some 750 men the *Oriole* moved out to an anchorage where *Plinlimmon* was waiting and the two crews simply changed places.

This time *Oriole* sailed at 2000 in the evening and was off Dunkirk just after midnight being ordered to wait to the east of the harbour where some 50 men, including French and Dutch troops, were picked-up from small craft. *Oriole* set sail at 0220 with two disabled motor boats in tow and reached Margate at 1305 on 4th June, by which time 'Operation Dynamo' had officially ended. The *Plinlimmon's* sister ship *Britannia*, then *HMS Skiddaw*, was in dock undergoing boiler cleaning at Rosyth when the evacuation started, emerging to set sail for Harwich on 31st May but arrived too late to take an active part.

The *Plinlimmon* returned to minesweeping duties off the North East Coast but was converted in London Docks to operate as an anti aircraft vessel during 1942, finishing the war as an accommodation ship in Harwich. Moved to lay-up on the Thames, the vessel was seriously damaged by fire in August 1946 and after being handed back to Campbells by the Director of Sea Transport in this condition, was deemed not worth reconditioning and sold for breaking-up at Grays, Essex, a process aided by a further fire in December 1946.

Having left our paddle minesweeper *Devonia* on the beach north of Dunkirk during the evacuation of the British Expeditionary Force in mid-1940, it was leave and back to Devonport. Word got around that a paddle minesweeper by the romantic name of *Lorna Doone* was fitted out and ready to take her wartime place helping to keep the coastal shipping lanes clear. So it was that several of the *Devonia* crew requested a draft to this ex-pleasure steamer with the attractive name. I soon found that she would command not only all the respect, love and affection that I was prepared to lavish on her, but also that of the other members of the crew. We found her to be a gracious lady of some fifty years, built, or a we preferred it, born on the Clyde in 1891 to serve people on pleasure trips in places as far apart as the Bristol Channel, Ilfracombe, Bournemouth, Isle of Wight, and even across the English Channel. Nevertheless, during compass swinging and sea trials she preened herself like a young maiden. One could hardly believe her age and that she had given similar service during the First World War.

She seemed to know where she was going and what would be expected of her and, as if to prove to her youthful crew that she at least knew what she was about, showed how well she could behave, even with a moderate sea running - and what a good turn of speed the engines could produce. I later learned that she was capable of 17.5 knots. Day by day, our confidence in her grew, and we all came to regard her as a 'lucky ship'. For those not used to paddle ships, they are a type requiring a good Captain and helmsman, for they are as much affected by wind as by tide, and when on the wheel one knew the challenge. You had to anticipate all her whims to follow the call of wind and tide. In a 'beam on' sea, she would roll slowly to be brought to a sudden halt as the sponson thumped the water's surface, then slowly heel over the other way until the opposite sponson served to halt the roll again. Engineers and stokers nursed her

engines and boilers with loving care, and peering into the inner sanctum of her 'heart' one could see them, oil can in one hand and cloth in the other, giving the shining well-engineered parts a wee drink and a wipe, as though smoothing the sweat from her brow. They knew full well that on the efficient working of those pistons and crankshafts our lives might well depend. I looked on our Chief Engineer as the doctor, giving her inner parts a regular medical

The stokers, all ex-Merchant Navy, known in their RN role as T124X, knew just how to feed her hungry belly. They were all tough men, such as 'Sham' Issacs. Later, Royal Navy stokers, mainly hostilities only ratings, took over. One Welshman, Edwards, with a wonderful tenor voice and quite unaware of his gift, usually sang when he thought he was alone with his beloved boilers. One would hear his marvellous voice reverberating from below, classic or ballad coming with equal ease, and we would listen and marvel. *Lorna* I am sure, thought he was singing for her alone. Yes, the crew were happy and *Lorna* was a happy ship. After working up, we had joined the Harwich Flotilla of paddle minesweepers. Ugly Ducklings of the Royal Navy they may have been, but to us *Lorna* was a swan and, like the rest of her breed, performed her duties with

Lorna Doone (J135) lying at Harwich with fellow south coast paddle steamers, *Emperor of India* and Red Funnel fleet-mate *Balmoral.* Of the trio, only *Emperor* of India returned to excursion sailings after the war *(IWM).*

just as much honour to her country as did the more impressive battleships, cruisers and destroyers. Our minesweeping duties round the Thames Estuary and north along the convoy route clearing mines dropped by aircraft and 'E' boats, were fairly routine, interrupted by odd planes makine low-level machine gun and bomb attacks. The crew came to regard the German plane crews as 'not too bright'. A couple of times 'Lord Haw-Haw' claimed that our *'Lorna'* had been sunk. The cheek of the man! It wasn't possible. Our lovely old lady bore a charmed life.

The crew was a pretty mixed bunch, RN, RNR, RNVR and others who were 'Hostilities Only,' but they all got on well together. There were men from Stornoway and fishermen from Hull, all fearless seamen from whom I learned a great deal. To mention specific individuals would take to long, for they were all characters in their own right. P.O. Torpedo Coxswain MacKenzie, RN, had trained the ship's cat who should have been called Calver, like a miniature tiger, having it jump from ledge to ledge in the mess. One day a seagull landed on deck and we watched as 'Tiger' stalked up and pounced on the sea-gulls back, teeth in it's neck. The poor bird flapped its wings and hurried along the deck manfully trying to take off, looking like a very overloaded Lancaster. At the last minute, 'Tiger' leapt off, letting the gull fly away. A little longer and he might have been the first cat to fly with it's own transport.

Our first C.O, by the name of Cook RN, had commanded minesweepers in the First War and was a peacetime Merchant Navy officer who may have come out of retirement. He was no spring chicken and was always very quiet. One day when returning to harbour we were to tie up a the coaling jetty. The fo'c'sle party were ready with heaving lines and fenders when, somehow, as we raced towards the jetty, we realised the C.O. was late with his helm and engine orders and as a man dropped everything and rushed aft. The C.O. having given his belated orders, leaned over the port wing and shouted 'get back, you cowards' as poor *Lorna Doone* ungraciously stuck her bow into the jetty, causing the crane above to shake rather ominously. Luckily the damage to the stem was slight. Of our first No 1, Ernie Fell said, with his true Hull humour: 'This one thinks work's a new kind of drink we should all enjoy'. On another day, we were secured alongside the Train-Ferry Jetty, painting ship. I was working on the bridge, carefully making sure all the final brush strokes were in the same direction. I removed the megaphone to paint behind it when suddenly I found my brush sweeping the mouthpiece, remembering of course that all final brush strokes should go the same way. Quite unexpectedly, the quartermaster piped 'Hands to stations for moving ship'. I hurried to my duties on the fo'c'sle and, looking up to the bridge, saw to my horror the C.O. picked up his megaphone and placed it to his mouth *'Let go aft,'* said he and, as he turned forward the lovely ring of battleship grey round his mouth cause subdued laughter. *'What are you laughing at, No 1?'* he bawled. *'Your face Sir'* said No 1. *'What the matter with my face?'* said the C.O. *'It's all paint, Sir,'* where upon the C.O. picked up a piece of rag from the voice-pipe to wipe off the offending paint, at the same time removing his hat in exasperation, just a passing seagull released his load right in the middle to his bald pate. There was more laughter as he shook his fist at the offender shouting loudly: *'All the bloody ocean, and you pick on me!'*

At first there was no let-up, but work from dawn to dusk. Being junior ship, we were last in line and often sweeping when a Dan Layer was not employed, the work of rigging, dropping and recovering these buoys usually fell to us. A Dan Buoy is a can on a pole, flag on top, weight at the bottom, with a sinker to hold it on the sea bed. The last ship in line of the sweep drops these at regular intervals to mark the area clearly, thus avoiding going over the same area twice. Consider that each Dan Buoy, when rigged, required six eyes in the wires and that our 'Jimmy' insisted on spliced eyes (instead of the easier way of two half hitches and a bull dog grip), and its easy to understand that we often had to work late into the night getting ready for a possible 5am start next day.

Recovering these buoys became an art. The faster we got them on board, the quicker we could return to harbour. With the last one on board, the stoker would really fill her hungry belly and *'Lorna'* would thrash the water with her blades, really showing her paces. Racing after the rest of the flotilla, a great broad wake streaming behind like a maiden's flowing tresses, we were seldom the last to tie up. When working, minesweepers were vulnerable to air attack, being unable to manoeuvre quickly, so a man was usually kept handy on the 'sweep deck' armed with an axe, ready to cut the wires if need be. On one occasion, when the ship was turned quickly and we steamed over our own sweep, a mine was caught, luckily horns down, as it bumped along the ship's bottom. The mine bobbed up under the stern, but a bit of clever veering and heaving the offender was cut adrift. It was quickly sunk by rifle fire.

On one day in harbour, the Coxswain had to explain to our 'Jimmy' that it was usual Navy practice on such a day to give a 'Make and Mend', in other words a half day off, to which he reluctantly agreed. This allowed the crew to catch up on hobbying, mending or sleeping. Naturally, most hands slung their hammocks and got their heads down, unless, of course, shore leave was given. We were operating with the fleet minesweepers on day when *HMS Fitzroy* struck a mine. 'Buzzer' - what else with a name like George Bee? - was there with his camera, unofficially, and got a good shot of the ship in a mountain of spray. Most of us managed to get a copy. *Lorna Doone* was fitted with a sickbay and carried the flotilla Medical Officer and a Leading Sickbay Attendant. 'Away lifeboat crew,' piped the Quartermaster, so with the medical pair aboard, Leading Seaman Carlisle as coxwain, and myself at stroke, the boat was lowered into the dropping position. The plug should have been in the starboard thwart knee, but wasn't. While searching for the 'sea keeper outer,' I stuck my finger in the hole, feeling rather like a famous Dutch boy. 'Slip,' came the order, and down we dropped into the slight swell. The fall hook failed to trip, so Spike Carlisle cleared it by hand trapping his thumb in the retaining catch as he did so. I watched helplessly as his thumb split and blood gushed forth. Spike gave no indication of his injury, other than wrapping his handkerchief tightly round the offending thumb. 'Give away together,' he ordered, and I finally found the plug and exchanged it for my frozen finger. The Doc and LSBA climbed aboard the *Fitzroy* to start work. The injured were mainly stokers scalded when steam pipes burst. First Aid over, those requiring treatment were taken on to our boat and the rest onto *Fitzroy's* whaler which

we towed back to *Lorna Doone*. Only after the injured from the *Fitzroy* had been cared for did L/S Carlisle get his own thumb attended to. I believe he received an Oak Leaf Clasp for his part in the work. The whaler was put on our deck and our heavy Board of Trade lifeboat was put ashore at Parkeston Quay, the whaler swung on the port davits in its place. We somehow obtained a mast and sails, so the crew were able to spend many pleasant off duty hours sailing the Rivers Stour and Orwell. We had also acquired a small motor boat for which the Chief Engineer obtained a small trawl. This meant regular supplies of fresh fish for the crew. Repairs to the net presented no problem at all with the Stornoway chaps on board and in fact it was from AB MacLeod that I learned the skill. It would seem that *Lorna Doone* may have been the only paddle boat in the fleet to sport both a motorboat and a whaler.

The time came when not many mines were being swept and plans had been made to build and position forts, like battleships on stilts resting on the sea-bed. Until these were on station, we had the job of providing guard over the Survey Vessels, and at night the ships of the flotilla anchored at various positions as A/A guard

Two war time views of *Lorna Doone*. The vessel is seen (left) at Plymouth when first commissioned in 1940 and (right) is seen leaving Newhaven. Although still carrying her anti-aircraft vessel pennant number the armament appears to have been removed, and the picture may have been taken in 1944 when the *Lorna Doone* was en route to the Clyde for use as an accommodation ship *(Richard Howarth collection).*

against mine-laying planes or 'E' boats. One night, a strange object was seen floating nearby. We didn't know what it was, or whether to shout at it or abandon ship. As the shape drifted nearer, it was seen to be a partially deflated barrage ballon. It was hauled aborad and most of the ships company cut off a section to take home as a souvenir. In the early hours of another morning, we on watch heard the coughing as spluttering of an engine. As it hove into view, it was seen to be one of our motor gun boats which had been doing battle and received some damage. Were they glad to see us! We were glad, too, to be able to give them what little assistance we could. There were numerous wrecks around the area, their masts and superstructure showing above the water. 'Lorna' along with several other ships, was near at hand when one merchantman sank. Cases and barrels of food were floating all over the place, so it was only natural that boats should be lowered for us to pick up all we could to add to our stores. About this time, Jerry was giving London and and other cities some stick each night. We at Harwich usually got the left-overs. On one occasion, as we were tied alongside what the locals called the Halfpenny Pier, a couple of bombs fell right between the jetty and our bows. the blast cause 'Lorna' to indignantly lift her bows some couple of feet, but the only damage was some broken crockery. Had we not had that paddle box keeping the bows some six feet from the jetty, then the bombs would have caused dear 'Lorna' considerable pain, but as I have already said, she led a charmed life. Our second C.O, Lieutenant Sherrin, a massive seemingly fearless six footer with a black beard, filled us with confidence and became so popular that I am sure we would have followed him into hell, if he said he could get us back. The flotilla used Lowestoft for tubes, back ends and boiler cleaning, and on each occasion half the ship's company were given leave in turn. Lowestoft was noted for the number of air-raid warnings it got per 24 hours. This was caused by single planes

Lorna Doone, with *Balmoral* outside, as accommodation and feeding vessels for personnel working in this floating dock on the Clyde in 1944
(Richard Howarth collection).

making hit-and-run low level machine-gun and bomb attacks. On one occasion, the watch aboard were painting ship and I was at the top of the mast when a lone raider came in low. The guns opened up showering bullets and shells at the raider, while I still clung to the top of the mast. I had never felt so alone. As the plane shot past me, I didn't know whether to throw my paint can at it or not.

Eventually the time came when the defence forts were in position and manned and it was decided that *Lorna Doone* would be fitted out for eating on board and another of our flotilla, the *Lorna Doone's* fleet mate *Balmoral,* for sleeping and sent to the Clyde to secure alongside a floating dock in Greenock as accommodation vessels for the workforce. Only six of the original crew were in the steaming party and the voyage round the coast was uneventful. Overnight stops were made at several ports and we arrived in the Clyde intact. Being acting coxswain for the trip I had the honour of taking the wheel for the last few miles, so I held 'Lorna's' hand to lead her back to the waters of her birth. She snuggled alongside the floating dock without a scratch and I looked around the wheelhouse for the last time. As a launch took the few of us and our kit to Gourock, we dare hardly look back lest a tear should find its way down a cheek. Yes, it was a sad day.

LAID-UP VESSELS REQUISITIONED

The Second World War can actually be said to have extended the working lives of some of the participating paddle steamers as they had been out of commission in the 1939 summer season and would probably not have been returned to commercial service. The New Medway Steam Packet laid-up sisters *Queen of Kent* and *Queen of Thanet,* and the veteran former Belle steamer *Essex Queen* in 1939 due to a combination of the depressed passenger market and the introduction of a new motor screw vessel. All three ships survived to return to commercial service; the Craigendoran favourite *Waverley* had been officially withdrawn by the LNER at the end of the 1938 season but remained laid-up at Bowling Harbour from where it was requisitioned almost as soon as the war started and was lost returning from Dunkirk; and at Southampton, mechanical trouble forced the Red Funnel company to withdraw the steamer *Bournemouth Queen.* It was not taken for conversion as an anti-aircraft vessel until 1942 but, still a coal burner, returned to excursion work until 1957.

Almost certainly the oldest quartet of Second World recruits were paddle veterans from the Cosens fleet whose ages in 1939 totalled 209 years! The oscillating engined *Empress* (1879) and *Victoria* (1884) were used on various duties in the Weymouth/Portland area until November 1944; the *Monarch*, dating from 1888, became *HMS Exway* and, based mainly at Devonport, served as an examination and contraband control vessel, a role in which she was both bombed and machine gunned from the air; while the *Consul* (1896) also served as a patrol and examination vessel from November 1939 to November 1944.

Immediately after the declaration of war there was a mass evacuation of children from London, a task mainly carried out by rail but for which the Thames excursion ships also played a part. In addition to the almost new motor vessels *Royal Daffodil, Royal Sovereign* and *Queen of the Channel* from the General Steam Navigation Company fleet, the paddle steamers *Royal Eagle, Crested Eagle, Golden Eagle* and *Thames Queen* all played their part in sailings to Great Yarmouth and Lowestoft. During this period *Crested Eagle* almost certainly made the last passenger call at the Claremont Pier, Lowestoft, when arriving with a full complement of children from the Dagenham area.

The oldest unit of the New Medway Steam Packet Company's fleet, the small paddle steamer *City of Rochester,* built on the Clyde in 1904, was taken up for service as a minesweeper and work was in progress before it was decided the vessel was unsuitable. It was then made into a naval stores carrier but was wrecked on 19th May 1941, on the eve of a first sailing from Chatham, when a mine dropped into the River Medway from a German aircraft exploded nearby. The hulk was beached and *City of Rochester* was demolished on the spot, therefore seeing no actual war service at all.

When, in 1937, Cosens and Co. bought the Portsmouth railway paddler *Duchess of Norfolk* for excursion work, their first choice of name, *Ambassador,* was not available and the vessel was introduced as *Embassy*. By a curious twist, when requisitioned for war service three years later, the *Embassy* became *HMS Ambassador!*

PRIESTLEY'S STEAMERS SAILING PROUDLY DOWN THE YEARS FROM THEIR EXCURSION TO HELL...

The *Gracie Fields* completed just four years of ferry and excursion work for Red Funnel before being lost returning from Dunkirk. The picture is thought to show the *Gracie Fields* approaching Bournemouth Pier during 1936 *(A.Duncan)*.

After the Dunkirk evacuation, the feeling of the British man in the street was admirably summed-up by J.B.Priestley in a programme following the BBC's main evening news on 5th June 1940. The Bradford-born writer and broadcaster, by then living on the South Coast, had been deeply moved by the part played in 'Operation Dynamo' by the now legendary 'little ships' and by the pleasure steamers in particular.

It was the day after Winston Churchill's historic 'We will fight them on the beaches...' address to parliament, repeated over the British Broadcasting Corporation's airwaves in the evening, in which he vowed the defence of the British Isles, whatever the cost. Priestley's own poignant address, is reproduced opposite:

The broadcast...

Nothing I feel could be more English than this Battle of Dunkirk, both in its end, its folly, its grandeur. It was very English in what sadly went wrong. Another such blunder may not be forgiven us. We have known these fussy little steamers and laughed at them all our lives. We called them 'the shilling slicks'. We watched them load and unload their crowds of holiday passengers - the gents full of high spirits and bottled beer, the ladies eating pork pies, the children sticky with peppermint rock. Sometimes they only went as far as the next seaside resort. But the boldest of them all might manage a Channel crossing. These *Brighton Queens* and *Brighton Belles* left that innocent foolish world of theirs to sail into the inferno, to defy bombs, shells, magnetic mines, and torpedoes to rescue our troops. Some of them, alas, like *Brighton Belle* and *Brighton Queen* will never return. Amongst them one I knew well, for it was the pride of our ferry service to the Isle of Wight - none other than the good ship *Gracie Fields*. I tell you, we were proud of the *Gracie Fields*, for she was the queen of our local line and instead of taking an hour over the voyage, she used to do it - churning like mad - in 45 minutes. And now, never again, will we board her at Cowes and go down into her dining saloon for a fine breakfast of bacon and eggs. She has paddled away for ever. But now, this little steamer, like all her brave sisters, badly battered, is immortal. She'll go sailing proudly down the years in the epic of Dunkirk. And yet our great grandchildren when they learn how we began this war by snatching glory out of defeat, and then swept on to victory, may also learn how the little holiday steamers made an excursion to hell and came back glorious.

J. B. Priestley, 1940

...and the steamer

When the *Gracie Fields* was built, the decision to name her after Britain's greatest entertainment star broke a long tradition of the Southampton company's ships having names with royal or local geographical association. It is also interesting to speculate why a paddle steamer, not so different in basic design and propulsion to vessels provided for Isle of Wight services before the 1914-18 war, was ordered for delivery as late as 1936 and some five years after a first diesel screw ferry had appeared at Southampton. When Gracie Fields launched the steamer, she led the crowds in a rendering of 'Sing as we go,' the title song from one of her hit films - and for which the screen play had been written by J.B.Priestley - as the vessel went down the Thornycroft slipway into the waters of the River Itchen at Woolston, Southampton. Soon after entering service the steamer went to Brighton to make a special cruise carrying Miss Fields and children from an orphanage she supported in the town. Later that season the *Gracie Fields* operated excursions from Bournemouth while the star was appearing there in a summer show.

The steamer was requisitioned in September 1939, joining the 10th Minesweeping Flotilla at Dover under the command of her peace-time skipper Captain N.R.Larkin who assumed the Royal Navy rank of Temporary Lieutenant. The steamer first crossed to Dunkirk on the evening of 27th May, at the start of 'Operation Dynamo.' After working off the beaches the *Gracie Fields* returned to Dover to land 281 men and then set sail for Dunkirk again, this time in company with the 10th Flotilla's Senior Officer's ship *Sandown* and the *Medway Queen*.

This time she succeeded in taking aboard some 750 men from the beaches at La Panne and was heading back and close to the Middel Kirk Buoy when attacked by Junkers 87 dive bombers. One of the bombs penetrated the engine room and both crew and troops were scalded by steam escaping from broken pipes. The rudder was also jammed and with no way of stopping the engine, the *Gracie Fields* circled at six knots. Two Dutch motor coasters, the *Jutland* and *Twente,* closed in and took off most of the troops. The minesweeper *Pangbourne,* itself damaged and laden with men, took off a further 80 and then attempted to tow *Gracie Fields.*

Gracie Fields pictured on patrol in the English Channel with flotilla
leader *Sandown. (J. D. Graves)*

Progress was painfully slow and eventually as the *Gracie Fields* filled with
water the line had to be cast off and remaining crew rescued before the ship
went down. Captain Larkin was among the survivors and he returned to
serve Red Funnel until retirement in 1961, commanding vessels including
the Southampton fleet's other Dunkirk participant, *Princess Elizabeth.*

One of the classic signals of the war was sent by Lieutenant Edwin Davies,
skipper of the paddle minesweeper *Oriole,* previously the Clyde steamer
Eagle III, during the Dunkirk evacuation. Even amid the chaos he found
time to advise the Admiralty: *"Deliberately grounded HMS Oriole,
Belgian coast, dawn on May 29th on own initiative, objective speedy
evacuation of troops. Refloated same day, no apparent damage. Meantime
am again proceeding to Belgian coast and will run aground again if such
course seems desirable."* The Admiralty's reply was equally to the point:
"Your action fully approved."

Usually the auxiliary anti-aircraft paddlers of the Thames flotilla sailed
independently, but on one occasion when the Senior Officer in *Royal
Eagle* led his ships to sea through the defence booms in line ahead, with the
coal fired *Laguna Belle* and *Thames Queen* belching smoke from their
funnels as they struggled to maintain position, one guard ship crew
member, responding to the sight, was heard to shout: "Blimey, old Hitler
must be trembling!".

Apart from Dunkirk, one of the more unusual rescue missions
undertaken during the Bristol Channel paddler *Glen Gower's* war service
followed a North Sea attack on a 3,000 ton Dutch cargo vessel loaded with
pit props. The paddler, which had been renamed *Glenmore* in 1941 and was
under the command of Lt. Cdr. Lachlan McLean-Sheddon, her P &
A.Campbell chief officer in the 1930s, managed to pick its way through a
seemingly endless sea of timber to get close enough to rescue 43 crew
members. On another occasion *Glenmore* towed the damaged *Laguna
Belle* towards the East Coast for several hours during which both vessels
were attacked by enemy aircraft.

The last paddler to be requisitioned for war service was the *Pioneer* from
the fleet of David MacBrayne, a vessel built on the Clyde in 1905 for service
to Islay from West Loch Tarbert. Taken by the Admiralty in March 1944,
the *Pioneer* was handed over in Greenock and proceeded to Fairlie and, as
HMS Harbinger, became headquarters ship for North Atlantic Submarine
Control. At the end of January 1945 the Admiralty bought the ship from
MacBrayne's for £15,000 and it was then fitted out for research work under
control of the Director of Submarine Warfare. A year later, the *Harbinger*
returned to the yard of A and J.Inglis, where it had been built, for the paddle
wheels to be removed prior to a tow to Portland Harbour and use as a
floating laboratory, a role that continued until 1958 when the vessel was
broken-up in Holland.

Pioneer, as *HMS Harbinger,* as an underwater detection and ASDIC
Training ship in Portland Harbour. *(Richard Howarth collection)*

A remarkable photograph of a mine detonating in the Firth of Forth during a sweep by the paddle minesweeper *Skiddaw* from the Granton-based 12th Flotilla. The photograph, from the Richard Howarth collection, is thought to have been taken in 1940 and shows the steamer near Inchkeith Island. *Skiddaw,* the Campbell favourite *Britannia,* completed in 1896, still has her foremast in its original position before it was moved in front of the bridge to allow extra anti-aircraft weapons to be fitted. The *Britannia* returned to excursion service in 1946 but encountered boiler troubles and was not in operation again until 1948 when re-appearing with a new boiler and twin funnels. In 1948, 1949 and 1950 the vessel spent the summer running on the Sussex coast and remained in the Bristol Channel fleet until withdrawn in the autumn of 1956 and towed away for scrap in December that year.

AN EMPEROR ANSWERS THE CALL

The *Emperor of India* looks particularly imposing in the picture opposite when the armament and pennant number indicate that it was taken after conversion to anti-aircraft vessel towards the end of 1940 - and perhaps after July 1943 following a switch to harbour duties as an accommodation ship. Despite never being regarded as a wholly satisfactory steamer, the *Emperor of India* served in peace and war for half a century before being broken-up in Belgium during 1957. Ordered originally for the Southampton, Isle of Wight and South of England Royal Mail Steam Packet Company, and to have been named *Princess Royal,* it was rejected and returned to builders Thornycroft for not meeting contract requirements, particularly in relation to speed. After rebuilding including lengthening and repositioning of the engine, it re-appeared in 1908 and joined the fleet of Cosens and Co. of Weymouth as *Emperor of India* and, prior to 1914, sometimes handled Cosens' cross-Channel trips to Cherbourg but was mainly employed on longer coastal cruises. After the start of the First World War she was requisitioned and served in the Eastern Mediterranean as a troop transport, hospital carrier and, later, as a minesweeper, initially as *HMS Emperor of India II* before the name was changed to *Mahratta.* Not released until 1920, the *Emperor of India* spent a couple of summers on charter to Sussex operators before being used as Cosens principal Bournemouth vessel throughout the 1930s. Quickly requisitioned in 1939, the *Emperor of India* joined the 10th Minesweeping Flotilla at Dover and took part in the Dunkirk evacuation, returning with a total of 642 troops. Although officially recorded operating under its own name, and when converted for A/A duties, there are also claims that the steamer was renamed

Bunting for the latter part of the war. Handed back to Cosens in May 1946, it was much altered before returning to service in July 1948 with a new funnel and wheelhouse and conversion to burn oil fuel. The saloons were superbly refitted with timber panelling including teak from a houseboat once owned by Lily Langtry but speed, never the *'Emperor's'* strong-point, dropped still further and at one stage she suffered the ignominy of being taken off long trips and used on the Bournemouth-Swanage service. The steamer's survival until the end of the 1956 season was, therefore, surprising.

Emperor of India arriving in Dover from Dunkirk in the early stages of 'Operation Dynamo' at the end of May 1940
(Times Newspapers)

SOME OF THE WAR'S FERRY STALWARTS

There was equal pressure on other routes to the Isle of Wight. Red Funnel's *Duchess of Cornwall* (above) has a few cars on her foredeck approaching Cowes and (below) there's little space to spare on the deck of the little *Solent* as it arrives at Yarmouth from Lymington on the Southern Railway route.

It was left to older steamers like the *Merstone* to keep open the Portmouth-Ryde service. The 1928-built paddler worked virtually non-stop for six years and also acted as a tender carrying troops to vessels in the Solent prior to the Normandy Landings. Here, in her drab wartime grey, *Merstone* approaches Ryde Pier, the foredeck filled with skips containing parcels, mail sacks and even milk churns.

The sterling service of some of the Isle of Wight ferry veterans was matched on the Clyde by steamers like the *Lucy Ashton* (above) which shouldered the burden of keeping open services from Craigendoran almost single handed. On the right, the LNER's Clyde Coast winter timetable for 1940/41, still offering full first and second class catering facilities for breakfast, luncheon and high tea!
After a number of years in the excursion trade on the Forth, the war brought the *Fair Maid* back to the Clyde and the steamer is seen in the Gareloch towards the end of 1939. although officially a decontamination ship, it made some passenger sailings.
These pictures and timetable come from the Richard Howarth collection.

TRAIN AND STEAMER SERVICES

CLYDE COAST
VIA
CRAIGENDORAN

WEEKDAYS
28th OCTOBER 1940
until further notice

Sc. 135

PRINTED IN GREAT BRITAIN

Medway Queen dry docked during her minesweeping days in a view thought to date from 1941 *(MQPS)*

THE SURVIVORS

Just three of the many paddle steamers which served during the Second World War survived to see the 50th anniversary of the end of hostilities. None of them have sailed commercially since the 1960s and, of the trio, only the *Princess Elizabeth*, preserved in Paris, appears to have an assured future. A £4m project to return the *Medway Queen* to service on the Thames has just been announced but at present there seems little prospect of the deterioration of the *Ryde*, marooned in the Isle of Wight, being halted.

Medway Queen

After cheating enemy bombers and artillery in seven epic crossings to Dunkirk in 1940, escaping from the threat of the breakers' yard on more than one occasion and overcoming the ravages of wind and weather, efforts to save the *Medway Queen* have reached a crossroads. The Medway Queen Preservation Society believes it has done as much as it can to keep the 71 year-old vessel in a condition from which full restoration is possible and everything now depends on the implementation of a rebuilding and recommissioning plan costing almost £4m. This would see the steamer returned to revenue earning service on the Thames from London.

The Medway Queen Foundation believes this last example of a Thames Estuary excursion paddle steamer could be viable running several tourist cruises a day from Tower Pier or St. Katharine's Pier to the Thames Barrier and back, with occasional longer trips for enthusiasts to old stamping grounds like Southend, Clacton on Sea or into the River Medway. But huge sums of money will have to be raised to turn dreams into reality and it is being emphasised that time is running out as the ship cannot be kept in its present condition indefinitely.

After the war ended, the *Medway Queen,* built at Troon by the Ailsa Shipbuilding Company, returned to service from the Medway towns to Southend with cruises on alternating days to Herne Bay or Clacton and continued uneventfully until withdrawn in 1963. Hopes of preservation as a Thames-side restaurant fell through and the ship had been sold to Belgian breakers before a group from the Isle of Wight secured it as the centrepiece of a marina project at Binfield on the River Medina between East Cowes and Newport.

This prospered for a period, although by 1980 the vessel was almost derelict and had to be returned to the Medway on a submersible pontoon. The Medway Queen Preservation Society then came into its own and after establishing the ship at a base at Damhead Creek on the Hoo Peninsular in 1987, successfully embarked on a holding operation to keep the *Medway Queen* afloat and undertake general cleaning and minor restoration works pending a full scale operation.

Local authority support enabled detailed structural surveys to be undertaken which revealed that the *Medway Queen's* fabric has survived sufficiently well for a return to operation to be considered a practical possibility. Now the emphasis is switching to raising the money for a massive exercise that will need a new boiler and auxiliary generators, substantial replacement of steelwork and total refitting of the passenger areas to modern catering standards.

Princess Elizabeth

Central Paris might seem an unlikely place for a British paddle steamer to end its days in tranquil retirement but this is where the *Princess Elizabeth* is now established by the Association de Defenses des Arts Typogaphiques as a museum and conference centre, moored at the Pont Mirabeau, as pictured by Alistair Deayton above. ADAT opened the 1927-built former member of the Southampton-based Red Funnel fleet in 1991 following two years of restoration work in Roeun. Previously the *Princess Elizabeth* had been in a static role on the River Thames, opening at a berth below Tower Bridge in 1970 and exactly 30 years to the hour of its last departure with troops from Bray Beach near Dunkirk.

In 1973 the *Princess Elizabeth* was moved upstream above London Bridge to a new berth at Old Swan Pier and remained there until 1987 when reported to have been acquired to fulfil a new role as a yacht club headquarters at Gravesend. This fell through and after being put on the market again the vessel was bought by the French graphical organisation.

Princess Elizabeth's early years included both excursion work and Southampton-Cowes ferry sailings when cars were carried on the open foredeck. After returning to Red Funnel in 1946, the steamer continued until 1959 when sold out of the fleet to put in a further six summers of South Coast excursion work for three different operators. It had been sold for scrap and the engine and boiler removed before being rescued and moved to the Thames.

Medway Queen in with flags flying on 27th April 1995, the day a major restoration project was announced *(Russell Plummer)*.

Ryde

The last paddle steamer to run between Portsmouth and the Isle of Wight, the *Ryde* was withdrawn in September 1969 and a year later arrived at Binfield to join the *Medway Queen*. The *Ryde* had been requisitioned for service as a minesweeper in 1940 and went to the 7th Flotilla at Granton, later being converted to anti-aircraft ship with service including a role in the Normandy Landings. It was returned to the Southern Railway in February 1946 but played a decreasing part in the ferry service after the introduction of new motor vessels.

After reaching Binfield the boiler was removed to create additional space but the triple diagonal engine, by builders Denny Brothers of Dumbarton, remains in place. Named *Ryde Queen,* the steamer effectively replaced *Medway Queen* as the site's main ship and suffered fire damage in 1977 when in use as a discotheque. During 1991 things looked more optimistic when the latest in a succession of owners made contact with the Paddle Steamer Preservation Society and some hull plating was replaced and plans for full static restoration were announced. Alas, by 1992, contact between the two parties broke down and with no work done since the structure of the *Ryde* has further deteriorated and the chances of the ship ever escaping from imprisonment in the Binfield mud are now remote.

TRADITIONS MAINTAINED

The proud tradition of coastal steamer cruising fostered during the hey day of many of the vessels featured in these pages, and before, continues to be upheld around the British Isles thanks to the longstanding efforts and influence of the Paddle Steamer Preservation Society. Founded in 1959 and now a Registered Charity, the Society is owner, through associated owning and operating companies of two paddle steamers, the *Waverley,* built in 1947 to replace the Clyde vessel of the same lost in 1940 during the evacuation of Dunkirk, and the former River Dart steamer *Kingswear Castle,* built in 1924 yet powered by engines dating from 1904.

The *Waverley* is now sailing through a 21st season of operational preservation and, in addition to a main summer season on the Firth of Clyde, visits other areas each Spring and Autumn and in 1990 crossed to Dunkirk to play a part in events to commemorate the 50th anniversary of the evacuation. In 1994 the steamer was in the Solent for the Naval Review to mark the 50th anniversary of the Normandy landings. *Kingswear Castle,* based at Chatham Historic Dockyard and performing a full programme of excursions on the Rivers Medway and Thames, has won the 1995 Scania Transport Trust Award for the excellence of its restoration. Since 1986 the motor vessel *Balmoral* has operated in support of the steamers spending summers on the Bristol Channel and making early and late season appearances in other areas.

Information regarding sailings by *Waverley* and *Balmoral* can be obtained from Waverley Excursions at either Gwalia Buildings, Barry Docks, South Glamorgan (Tel: 01446-720656) or the Waverley Terminal, Glasgow (Tel: 0141-2218152). For *Kingswear Castle* contact Kingswear Castle Excursions, Historic Dockyard, Chatham (Tel: 01634-827648). Paddle Steamer Preservation Society membership information is available aboard all three vessels, or from the Subscription Secretary, PO Box 385, Hazlemere, High Wycombe, Bucks, HP11 1AG.

Medway Queen Preservation Society information is available from the membership Secretary, 72 Bells Lane, Hoo Saint Werburgh, Rochester, Kent, ME3 9HU.

ACKNOWLEDGEMENTS

The appearance of this book to commemorate the part played by paddle excursion vessels and ferries in the Second World War is due to the support, both directly and indirectly, of a large number of individuals. Thanks are due to Waverley chairman Terry Sylvester for the initial concept and much practical help and encouragement during production, together with welcome photographic contributions from their own collections by Victor Gray, Chris Collard, Nick James, Nigel Coombes, Richard Clammer, Martin Oatway, Marshall Vine and, particularly Richard Howarth. We are also extremely grateful to Mrs Jean Cameron, widow of Captain John Cameron, DSM, for making available the broadcast script that forms the basis of the fascinating Scottish Paddlers chapter, and to John Crosby for use of the photographs taken at Dunkirk by his late father J.Rutherford Crosby. Other articles have been adapted from issues of the Paddle Steamer Preservation Society journal 'Paddle Wheels.'

I would also like to express personal appreciation for the support and professional expertise of Graham Simons of GMS Enterprises and printers Woolnough Ltd which enabled the project to be completed from inception to publication in just two months. Every effort has been made to check the accuracy of the information contained but records in the period 1939-45 were not always complete and after half a century and more, individual memories can fade. I would be pleased to receive additional information relating to any of the vessels in the foregoing pages via the Waverley Excursions office in Barry.

Russell Plummer
May 1995.